THE ORCHARD
BOOK *of* POEMS

THE ORCHARD
BOOK *of* POEMS

Chosen by ADRIAN MITCHELL

Illustrated by CHLOE CHEESE

ORCHARD BOOKS

This book is especially for my beloved extra daughter

Boty Goodwin and in happy memory of her real mother and father —

Pauline Boty and Clive Goodwin.

First published in Great Britain in 1993 by
ORCHARD BOOKS
96 Leonard Street, London EC2A 4RH
Orchard Books Australia
14 Mars Road, Lane Cove, NSW 2066
Selection © Adrian Mitchell 1993
Illustrations © Chloe Cheese 1993
The right of Adrian Mitchell to be identified as author of this work and
of Chloe Cheese as illustrator has been asserted by them in accordance with
the Copyright, Designs and Patents Act, 1988.
A CIP catalogue record for this book is available from the British Library.
1 85213 316 3
Printed in Great Britain by The Bath Press

CONTENTS

1. THE PALACE OF PEOPLE

2. THE BURNING DESERT AND THE COOL ORCHARD

CONTENTS

3. THE VALLEY OF ANIMALS

CONTENTS

CONTENTS

7. THE SPELLBOUND MOUNTAIN

Welcome to Poetry

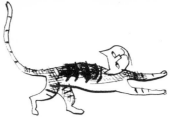

Poetry began in the days when everyone lived in caves or forests. Long before writing was invented, people would make up poems — love poems, hate poems, poems to make the crops grow or the rain fall. These poems were usually sung and danced by tribes. Every tribe made up its own poems. They all needed poetry.

Nowadays some people live without poetry. They're missing just as much as people who live without music.

I began to love poetry when I was about two. My Mother and Father would tuck me up in bed and read me poems or sing me songs with one arm around me. So poetry made me feel safe and warm and loved.

At the age of eight I recited a poem in public for the first time. It was the ballad of Sir Patrick Spens, which you'll find in this book. I borrowed my Father's Scottish accent for the performance which thrilled me twice as much as the audience.

I started writing poems and plays at the age of nine, and nobody has been able to stop me. At about the same age I was given the Golden Treasury, a wonderful anthology of poems which I read endlessly. I didn't understand all the poems, but I could enjoy their music.

Pick a poem, any poem, and read it to yourself. If you like it, try reading it aloud. If it sounds good, learn it by heart. It'll stay in your heart and you can use that poem whenever you need it.

When I chose the poems for the book I thought of poetry as
an exciting island, with valleys full of animals and palaces
packed with people. Maybe it's a slightly foreign island,
sometimes dangerous, sometimes magical or ridiculous —
poetry is a wild island well worth exploring.

The Orchard Book of Poems includes poems of all kinds — old
ones, new ones, mild ones, happy ones, sad ones, daft ones,
rough ones and gentle ones. Some of them rhyme and some of
them don't — but they all have rhythm and they all have a touch
of magic which excites me. A few of them were written specially
for children. But most of them were written for everybody.
They'll last you a lifetime. The same poem may mean one thing
when you're nine, another thing when you're nineteen and yet
another thing when you're ninety-nine.

*Reader: But what **is** Poetry?*
Adrian:

Poetry is a beautiful mud-pie
Washed down with a glassful of stars.

Poetry is one of the best ways
Of singing to the whole wide world
Or whispering in the ear of your best friend.

Poetry tunnels you out of your dungeon.
Poetry captures the three-headed dragon.
And teaches it Ludo and Frisbee-throwing.

Poetry is a Mammoth in a shopping mall,
A beggar with no legs in Disneyland,
A chocolate bicycle,
A truthburger with French flies
And the Moon's own telephone.

Poetry is your mind dancing
To the drumbeat of your heart.

Adrian Mitchell

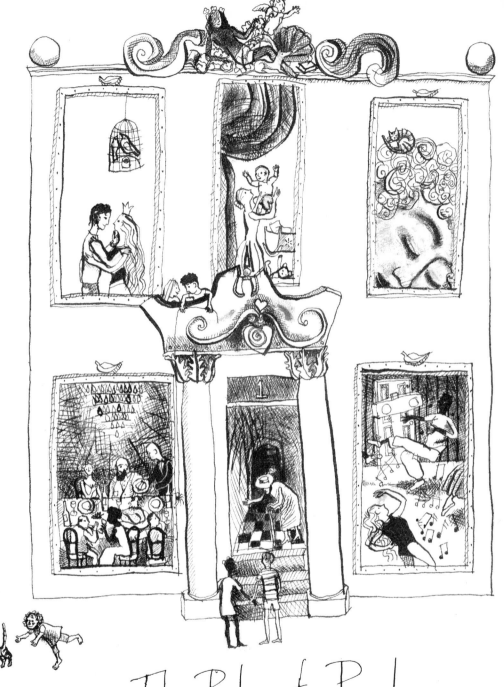

The Palace of People

Births and Deaths   Love and Friendship

Youth and Age

Crimson Curtains

Crimson curtains round my mother's bed,
   Silken soft as may be;
Cool white curtains round about my bed,
   For I am but a baby.

Christina Rossetti

Motherless Baby

Motherless baby and babyless mother,
Bring them together to love one another.

Christina Rossetti

I Remember, I Remember

I remember, I remember,
The house where I was born,
The little window where the sun
Came peeping in at morn;
He never came a wink too soon,
Nor brought too long a day,
But now, I often wish the night
Had borne my breath away!

I remember, I remember,
The roses, red and white,
The violets, and the lily-cups,
Those flowers made of light!
The lilacs where the robin built,
And where my brother set
The laburnum on his birthday –
The tree is living yet!

I remember, I remember,
Where I was used to swing,
And thought the air must rush as fresh
To swallows on the wing;
My spirit flew in feathers then,
That is so heavy now,
And summer pools could hardly cool
The fever on my brow!

I remember, I remember,
The fir trees dark and high;
I used to think their slender tops
Were close against the sky:
It was a childish ignorance,
But now 'tis little joy
To know I'm farther off from Heav'n
Than when I was a boy.

Thomas Hood

First Day at School

A millionbillionwillion miles from home
Waiting for the bell to go. (To go where?)
Why are they all so big, other children?
So noisy? So much at home they
must have been born in uniform
Lived all their lives in playgrounds
Spent the years inventing games
that don't let me in. Games
that are rough, that swallow you up.

And the railings.
All around, the railings.
Are they to keep out wolves and monsters?
Things that carry off and eat children?
Things you don't take sweets from?
Perhaps they're to stop us getting out
Running away from the lessins. Lessin.
What does a lessin look like?
Sounds small and slimy.
They keep them in glassrooms.
Whole rooms made out of glass. Imagine.

I wish I could remember my name
Mummy said it would come in useful.
Like wellies. When there's puddles.
Yellowwellies. I wish she was here.
I think my name is sewn on somewhere
Perhaps the teacher will read it for me.
Tea-cher. The one who makes the tea.

Roger McGough

The School-Boy

I love to rise in a summer morn
When the birds sing on every tree;
The distant huntsman winds his horn,
And the sky-lark sings with me:
O, what sweet company!

But to go to school in a summer morn,
O! it drives all joy away;
Under a cruel eye outworn
The little ones spend the day
In sighing and dismay.

Ah! then at times I drooping sit,
And spend many an anxious hour;
Nor in my book can I take delight,
Nor sit in learning's bower,
Worn through with the dreary shower.

How can the bird that is born for joy
Sit in a cage and sing?
How can a child when fears annoy
But droop his tender wing,
And forget his youthful spring?

O! Father and Mother, if buds are nipped,
And blossoms blown away,
And if the tender plants are stripped
Of their joy in the springing day
By sorrow and care's dismay,

How shall the summer arise in joy
Or the summer fruits appear?
Or how shall we gather what griefs destroy
Or bless the mellowing year,
When the blasts of winter appear?

William Blake

1945

The news was of inhumanity,
Of crimes, obscenities,
Unspeakable insanity
And bestial atrocities.

Somebody turned the radio down.
Nobody said a word.
Auschwitz, Buchenwald, and Belsen:
"It couldn't happen here," they said.

At school the teacher set revision:
Of the princes murdered in the tower,
The Spanish Inquisition,
And Genghis Khan drunk with power;

Of heretics, burnt at the stake,
Refusing to deny a vow;
Mass-murders for religion's sake;
He said, "It couldn't happen now."

"You're next," the school bullies snigger,
"Don't try any silly tricks!"
All through History he tries to figure
A way out of punches and kicks.

At the end of morning school,
They drag him to an air-raid shelter.
Down into darkness, damp and cool,
With Puncher and Kicker and Belter.

They tear off all his clothes
And tread them on the floor.
With obscenities and oaths,
They let him have what-for.

Their tortures are very crude,
Clumsy and unrefined.
With a sudden change of mood
They pretend to be friendly and kind.

They change their tack once more
And punch him black and blue.
He ends, crouched on the floor,
And finally they're through.

With a special parting kick
They warn him not to talk.
He feels wretched, sore and sick,
Gets up, can hardly walk.

It's a beautiful Summer day,
His eyes squint in the sun.
He hears two passing women say,
"Oh, schooldays are such fun."

Words echo in his head:
"Couldn't happen here," they said.
And "Couldn't happen now," they said.
He never breathes a word.

Geoffrey Summerfield

It Was Long Ago

I'll tell you, shall I, something I remember?
Something that still means a great deal to me.
It was long ago.

A dusty road in summer I remember,
A mountain, and an old house, and a tree
That stood, you know,

Behind the house. An old woman I remember
In a red shawl with a grey cat on her knee
Humming under a tree.

She seemed the oldest thing I can remember,
But then perhaps I was not more than three.
It was long ago.

I dragged on the dusty road, and I remember
How the old woman looked over the fence at me
And seemed to know

How it felt to be three, and called out, I remember
"Do you like bilberries and cream for tea?"
I went under the tree

And while she hummed, and the cat purred, I remember
How she filled a saucer with berries and cream for me
So long ago,

Such berries and such cream as I remember
I never had seen before, and never see
Today, you know.

And that is almost all I can remember,
The house, the mountain, the grey cat on her knee,
Her red shawl, and the tree,

And the taste of the berries, the feel of the sun I remember,
And the smell of everything that used to be
So long ago,

Till the heat on the road outside again I remember,
And how the long dusty road seemed to have for me
No end, you know.

That is the farthest thing I can remember.
It won't mean much to you. It does to me.
Then I grew up, you see.

Eleanor Farjeon

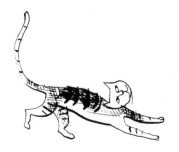

Fantasy of an African Boy

Such a peculiar lot
we are, we people
without money, in daylong
yearlong sunlight, knowing
money is somewhere, somewhere.

Everybody says it's a big
bigger brain bother now,
money. Such millions and millions
of us don't manage at all
without it, like war going on.

And we can't eat it. Yet
without it our heads alone
stay big, as lots and lots do,
coming from nowhere joyful,
going nowhere happy.

We can't drink it up. Yet
without it we shrivel when small
and stop for ever
where we stopped,
as lots and lots do.

We can't read money for books.
Yet without it we don't
read, don't write numbers,
don't open gates in other countries,
as lots and lots never do.

We can't use money to bandage
sores, can't pound it
to powder for sick eyes
and sick bellies. Yet without
it, flesh melts from our bones.

Such walled-round gentlemen
overseas minding money! Such
bigtime gentlemen, body guarded
because of too much respect
and too many wishes on them:

too many wishes, everywhere,
wanting them to let go
magic of money, and let it fly
away, everywhere, day and night,
just like dropped leaves in wind!

James Berry

Luchin

Fragile as a kite
over the roofs of Barrancas
little Luchin was playing
his hands blue with cold,
with his rag ball
the cat and the dog
and the horse looked on.

Green light was bathing
in the water of his eyes.
Bare-bummed and in the mud
His little life spent crawling
with the rag ball the cat and the dog
and the horse looked on.

His eyes brimming pools of green,
his brief life spent crawling,
little bare bottom in the mud.

The horse was another toy
in that tiny space
and it seemed that the animal
understood his job,
with the rag ball
the cat and the dog
and with Luchin wet through.

If there are children like Luchin
who are eating earth and worms,
let's open all the cages,
so they can fly away like birds
with the rag ball the cat and the dog
and with the horse as well.

Victor Jara

Fern Hill

Now as I was young and easy under the apple boughs
About the lilting house and happy as the grass was green,
   The night above the dingle starry,
     Time let me hail and climb
    Golden in the heydays of his eyes,
And honoured among wagons I was prince of the apple towns
And once below a time I lordly had the trees and leaves
     Trail with daisies and barley
    Down the rivers of the windfall light.

And as I was green and carefree, famous among the barns
About the happy yard and singing as the farm was home,
   In the sun that is young once only,
     Time let me play and be
    Golden in the mercy of his means,
And green and golden I was huntsman and herdsman, the calves
Sang to my horn, the foxes on the hills barked clear and cold,
     And the sabbath rang slowly
    In the pebbles of the holy streams.

All the sun long it was running, it was lovely, the hay
Fields high as the house, the tunes from the chimneys, it was air
    And playing, lovely and watery
     And fire green as grass.
    And nightly under the simple stars
As I rode to sleep the owls were bearing the farm away,
All the moon long I heard, blessed among stables, the nightjars
    Flying with the ricks, and the horses
     Flashing into the dark.

And then to awake, and the farm, like a wanderer white
With the dew, come back, the cock on his shoulder: it was all
    Shining, it was Adam and maiden,
        The sky gathered again
      And the sun grew round that very day.
So it must have been after the birth of the simple light
In the first, spinning place, the spellbound horses walking warm
    Out of the whinnying green stable
        On to the fields of praise.

And honoured among foxes and pheasants by the gay house
Under the new-made clouds and happy as the heart was long,
    In the sun born over and over,
        I ran my heedless ways,
    My wishes raced through the house high hay
And nothing I cared, at my sky blue trades, that time allows
In all his tuneful turning so few and such morning songs
    Before the children green and golden
        Follow him out of grace,

Nothing I cared, in the lamb white days, that time would take me
Up to the swallow-thronged loft by the shadow of my hand,
    In the moon that is always rising,
        Nor that riding to sleep
    I should hear him fly with the high fields
And wake to the farm forever fled from the childless land.
Oh as I was young and easy in the mercy of his means,
        Time held me green and dying
    Though I sang in my chains like the sea.

Dylan Thomas

About Friends

The good thing about friends
is not having to finish sentences.

I sat a whole summer afternoon with my friend
    once
on a river bank, bashing heels on the baked mud
and watching the small chunks slide into the
    water
and listening to them – plop plop plop.
He said "I like the twigs when they…
    you know…
like that." I said "There's that branch…"
We both said "Mmmm". The river flowed and
    flowed
and there were lots of butterflies, that afternoon.

I first thought there was a sad thing about
    friends
when we met twenty years later.
We both talked hundreds of sentences,
taking care to finish all we said,
and explain it all very carefully,
as if we'd been discovered in places
we should not be, and were somehow ashamed.

I understood then what the river meant by
    flowing.

Brian Jones

Poem For My Sister

My little sister likes to try my shoes,
to strut in them,
admire her spindle-thin twelve-year-old legs
in this season's styles.
She says they fit her perfectly,
but wobbles
on their high heels, they're
hard to balance.

I like to watch my little sister
playing hopscotch, admire the neat hops-and-skips of her,
their quick peck,
never missing their mark, not
overstepping the line.
She is competent at peever.

I try to warn my little sister
about unsuitable shoes,
point out my own distorted feet, the calluses,
odd patches of hard skin.
I should not like to see her
in my shoes.
I wish she should stay
sure-footed,
                    sensibly shod.

Liz Lochhead

Byes

it's sad when a person gets off the bus
and looks at the one who stayed on top to wave bye
and for the one on top to be looking elsewhere

it's sad when a person gets off the bus
and doesn't look at the one who stayed on top waving bye
and walks off looking as though miles away

it's great when a person gets off the bus
and peeps at the one who stayed on top
to wave bye
and the one on top peeps down
at the one going along the pavement miles away but half peeping
and they both discover each other and wave bye

it's a bore when a person gets off the bus
and waves bye bye to the one on top who
waves bye bye

are there other possible variations?
(do this for homework)

Mauricio Redoles

First Love

I ne'er was struck before that hour
    With love so sudden and so sweet.
Her face it bloomed like a sweet flower
    And stole my heart away complete.
My face turned pale as deadly pale,
    My legs refused to walk away,
And when she looked "what could I ail?"
    My life and all seemed turned to clay.

And then my blood rushed to my face
    And took my sight away.
The trees and bushes round the place
    Seemed midnight at noonday.
I could not see a single thing,
    Words from my eyes did start;
They spoke as chords do from the string
    And blood burnt round my heart.

Are flowers the winter's choice?
    Is love's bed always snow?
She seemed to hear my silent voice
    And love's appeal to know.
I never saw so sweet a face
    As that I stood before:
My heart has left its dwelling place
    And can return no more.

John Clare

Since First I Saw Your Face

Since first I saw your face, I resolved to honour and renown ye;
If now I be disdained, I wish my heart had never known ye.
What? I that loved and you that liked, shall we begin to wrangle?
No, no, no, my heart is fast, and cannot disentangle.

If I admire or praise you too much, that fault you may forgive me;
Or if my hands had strayed but a touch, then justly might you leave me
I asked you leave, you bade me love; is't now a time to chide me?
No, no, no, I'll love you still what fortune e'er betide me.

The sun, whose beams most glorious are, rejecteth no beholder,
And your sweet beauty past compare made my poor eyes the bolder;
Where beauty moves and wit delights and signs of kindness bind me,
There, O there, where'er I go I'll leave my heart behind me!

Anon

Without You

Without you every morning would be like going back to work
after a holiday,
Without you I couldn't stand the smell of the East Lancs Road,
Without you ghost ferries would cross the Mersey manned by
skeleton crews,
Without you I'd probably feel happy and have more money
and time and nothing to do with it,
Without you I'd have to leave my stillborn poems on other
people's doorsteps, wrapped in brown paper,
Without you there'd never be sauce to put on sausage butties,
Without you plastic flowers in shop windows would just be
plastic flowers in shop windows,
Without you I'd spend my summers picking morosely over
the remains of train crashes,
Without you white birds would wrench themselves free from
my paintings and fly off dripping blood into the night,
Without you green apples wouldn't taste greener,
Without you Mothers wouldn't let their children play out after tea,
Without you every musician in the world would forget how to
play the blues,
Without you Public Houses would be public again,
Without you the Sunday Times colour supplement would
come out in black-and-white,
Without you indifferent colonels would shrug their shoulders
and press the button,
Without you they'd stop changing the flowers in Piccadilly
Gardens,
Without you Clark Kent would forget how to become
Superman,

Without you Sunshine Breakfast would only consist of
Cornflakes,
Without you there'd be no colour in Magic colouring books,
Without you Mahler's 8th would only be performed by street
musicians in derelict houses,
Without you they'd forget to put the salt in every packet of crisps,
Without you it would be an offence punishable by a fine of up
to £200 or two months' imprisonment to be found in
possession of curry powder,
Without you riot police are massing in quiet sidestreets,
Without you all streets would be one-way the other way,
Without you there'd be no one not to kiss goodnight when we
quarrel,
Without you the first martian to land would turn round and go
away again,
Without you they'd forget to change the weather,
Without you blind men would sell unlucky heather,
Without you there would be
no landscapes/no stations/no houses,
no chipshops/no quiet villages/no seagulls
on beaches/no hopscotch on pavements/no night/no morning/
there'd be no city no country
Without you.

Adrian Henri

She Walks in Beauty

She walks in beauty, like the night
    Of cloudless climes and starry skies;
And all that's best of dark and bright
    Meet in her aspect and her eyes:
Thus mellow'd to that tender light
    Which heaven to gaudy day denies.

One shade the more, one ray the less,
    Had half impair'd the nameless grace
Which waves in every raven tress,
    Or softly lightens o'er her face;
Where thoughts serenely sweet express
    How pure, how dear their dwelling-place.

And on that cheek, and o'er that brow,
    So soft, so calm, yet eloquent,
The smiles that win, the tints that glow,
    But tell of days in goodness spent,
A mind at peace with all below,
    A heart whose love is innocent!

Lord Byron

Meeting at Night

The grey sea and the long black land;
And the yellow half-moon large and low;
And the startled little waves that leap
In fiery ringlets from their sleep,
As I gain the cove with pushing prow,
And quench its speed i' the slushy sand.

Then a mile of warm sea-scented beach;
Three fields to cross till a farm appears;
A tap at the pane, the quick sharp scratch
And blue spurt of a lighted match,
And a voice less loud, thro' its joys and fears,
Than the two hearts beating each to each!

Robert Browning

Like a Flame

Raising up
from my weeding
of ripening cane

my eyes
make four
with this man

there ain't
no reason
to laugh

but
I laughing
in confusion

his hands
soft his words
quick his lips
curling as in
prayer

I nod

I like this man

Tonight
I go to meet him
like a flame

Grace Nichols

How Long Blues

How long, baby, how long
Has that even' train been gone?
How long? How long? I say, How long?
Standin' at the station watchin' my baby leave town,
Sure am disgusted – for where could she be gone –
For how long? How long? I say, how long?

I can hear the whistle blowin' but I cannot see no train
And deep down in my heart I got an ache and pain
For how long? How long? I say, how long?

Sometimes I feel so disgusted and I feel so blue
That I hardly know what in this world it's best to do
For how long, how long, how long?

If I could holler like I was a mountain jack
I'd go up on the mountain and call my baby back.
For how long, how long, how long?

If some day she's gonna be sorry that she done me wrong
Baby, it will be too late then – for I'll be gone
For so long, so long, so long!

My mind gets to rattling, I feel so bad
Thinkin' 'bout the bad luck that I have had
For so long, so long, so long.

How long? Baby, how long?
Baby, how long?
How long?

Anon

The Enchanted Mistress

I met brightness of brightness upon the path of loneliness;
Plaiting of plaiting in every lock of her yellow hair.
News of news she gave me, and she as lonely as she was;
News of the coming back of him that owns the tribute of the king.

Folly of follies I to go so near to her,
Slave I was made by a slave that put me in hard bonds.
She made away from me then and I following after her
Till we came to a house of houses made by Druid enchantments.

They broke into mocking laughter, a troop of men of enchantments,
And a troop of young girls with smooth-plaited hair.
They put me up in chains, they made no delay about it –
And my love holding to her breast an awkward ugly clown.

I told her then with the truest words I could tell her,
It was not right for her to be joined with a common clumsy churl;
And the man that was three times fairer than the whole race of the Scots
Waiting till she would come to him to be his beautiful bride.

At the sound of my words her pride set her crying,
The tears were running down over the kindling of her cheeks.
She sent a lad to bring me safe from the place I was in.
She is the brightness of brightness I met in the path of loneliness.

Lady Gregory

I Gave My Love a Cherry

I gave my love a cherry without a stone;
I gave my love a chicken without a bone;
I gave my love a ring without an end;
I gave my love a baby with no crying.

How can there be a cherry without a stone?
How can there be a chicken without a bone?
How can there be a ring without an end?
How can there be a baby with no crying?

A cherry, when it's blooming, it has no stone;
A chicken, when it's pipping, it has no bone;
A ring, when it's rolling, it has no end;
A baby, when it's sleeping, has no crying.

Anon

Donall Oge

It is late last night the dog was speaking of you,
The snipe was speaking of you in her deep marsh.
It is you are the lonely bird throughout the woods,
And that you may be without a mate until you find me.

You promised me and you said a lie to me,
That you would be before me where the sheep are flocked.
I gave a whistle and three hundred cries to you,
And I found nothing there but a bleating lamb.

You promised me a thing that was hard for you,
A ship of gold under a silver mast,
Twelve towns and a market in all of them,
And a fine white court by the side of the sea.

You promised me a thing that is not possible,
That you would give me gloves of the skin of a fish,
That you would give me shoes of the skin of a bird,
And a suit of the dearest silk in Ireland.

My mother said to me not to be talking with you,
Today or tomorrow or on the Sunday.
It was a bad time she took for telling me that,
It was shutting the door after the house was robbed.

You have taken the east from me, you have taken the west from me,
You have taken what is before me and what is behind me;
You have taken the moon, you have taken the sun from me,
And my fear is great you have taken God from me.

Lady Gregory

A Red, Red Rose

O my Luve's like a red, red rose
    That's newly sprung in June:
O my Luve's like the melodie
    That's sweetly play'd in tune!

As fair art thou, my bonnie lass,
    So deep in luve am I:
And I will luve thee still, my dear,
    Till a' the seas gang dry:

Till a' the seas gang dry, my dear,
    And the rocks melt wi' the sun;
I will luve thee still, my dear,
    While the sands o' life shall run.

And fare thee weel, my only Luve,
    And fare thee weel a while!
And I will come again, my Luve,
    Tho' it were ten thousand mile.

Robert Burns

A Ditty

My true-love hath my heart, and I have his,
By just exchange one to the other given:
I hold his dear, and mine he cannot miss,
There never was a better bargain driven:
    My true-love hath my heart, and I have his.

His heart in me keeps him and me in one,
My heart in him his thoughts and senses guides:
He loves my heart, for once it was his own,
I cherish his because in me it bides:
    My true-love hath my heart, and I have his.

Sir Philip Sidney

A Poison Tree

I was angry with my friend:
I told my wrath, my wrath did end.
I was angry with my foe:
I told it not, my wrath did grow.

And I water'd it in fears,
Night and morning with my tears;
And I sunned it with smiles,
And with soft deceitful wiles.

And it grew both day and night,
Till it bore an apple bright;
And my foe beheld it shine,
And he knew that it was mine,

And into my garden stole
When the night had veil'd the pole:
In the morning glad I see
My foe outstretch'd beneath the tree.

William Blake

Love's Farewell

Since there's no help, come let us kiss and part –
Nay I have done, you get no more of me;
And I am glad, yea, glad with all my heart,
That thus so cleanly I myself can free;

Shake hands for ever, cancel all our vows,
And when we meet at any time again,
Be it not seen in either of our brows
That we one jot of former love retain.

Now at the last gasp of love's latest breath,
When his pulse failing, passion speechless lies,
When faith is kneeling by his bed of death,
And innocence is closing up his eyes,

– Now if thou woulds't, when all have given him over,
From death to life thou might'st him yet recover!

Michael Drayton

Helen of Kirconnell

I wish I were where Helen lies;
Night and day on me she cries;
O that I were where Helen lies
   On fair Kirconnell lea!

Curst be the heart that thought the thought,
And curst the hand that fired the shot,
When in my arms burd Helen dropt,
   And died to succour me!

O think na but my heart was sair
When my Love dropt down and spak nae mair!
I laid her down wi' meikle care
   On fair Kirconnell lea.

As I went down the waterside,
None but my foe to be my guide,
None but my foe to be my guide,
　　On fair Kirconnell lea;

I lighted down my sword to draw,
I hackéd him in pieces sma',
I hackéd him in pieces sma',
　　For her sake that died for me.

O Helen fair, beyond compare!
I'll make a garland of thy hair
Shall bind my heart for evermair
　　Until the day I die.

O that I were where Helen lies!
Night and day on me she cries;
Out of my bed she bids me rise,
　　Says, "Haste and come to me!"

O Helen fair! O Helen chaste!
If I were with thee, I were blest,
Where thou lies low and takes thy rest
　　On fair Kirconnell lea.

I wish my grave were growing green,
A winding-sheet drawn ower my een,
And I in Helen's arms lying,
　　On fair Kirconnell lea.

I wish I were where Helen lies;
Night and day on me she cries;
And I am weary of the skies,
　　Since my Love died for me.

Anon

A Birthday

My heart is like a singing bird
    Whose nest is in a water'd shoot;
My heart is like an apple tree
    Whose boughs are bent with thick-set fruit;
My heart is like a rainbow shell
    That paddles in a halcyon sea;
My heart is gladder than all these,
    Because my love is come to me.

Raise me a daïs of silk and down;
    Hang it with vair and purple dyes;
Carve it in doves and pomegranates,
    And peacocks with a hundred eyes;
Work it in gold and silver grapes,
    In leaves and silver fleurs-de-lys;
Because the birthday of my life
    Is come, my love is come to me.

Christina Rossetti

So We'll Go No More A Roving

So, we'll go no more a roving
    So late into the night,
Though the heart be still as loving,
    And the moon be still as bright.

For the sword outwears its sheath,
    And the soul wears out the breast,
And the heart must pause to breathe,
    And love itself have rest.

Though the night was made for loving,
And the day returns too soon,
Yet we'll go no more a roving
By the light of the moon.

Lord Byron

Warning

When I am an old woman I shall wear purple
With a red hat which doesn't go, and doesn't suit me.
And I shall spend my pension on brandy and summer gloves
And satin sandals, and say we've no money for butter.
I shall sit down on the pavement when I'm tired
And gobble up samples in shops and press alarm bells
And run my stick along the public railings
And make up for the sobriety of my youth.
I shall go out in my slippers in the rain
And pick the flowers in other people's gardens
And learn to spit.

You can wear terrible shirts and grow more fat
And eat three pounds of sausages at a go
Or only bread and pickle for a week
And hoard pens and pencils and beermats and things in boxes.

But now we must have clothes that keep us dry
And pay our rent and not swear in the street
And set a good example for the children.
We must have friends to dinner and read the papers.

But maybe I ought to practise a little now?
So people who know me are not too shocked and surprised
When suddenly I am old, and start to wear purple.

Jenny Joseph

53

Happiest Girl

Mrs Mary Leighton's 89-year-old body was as frail as a wigwam:
A house of bone she lived in, covered only by a stretch of skin
And a faint white dusting of talcum powder.
Somewhere in her body grew a rebellion of cells –
The ranks of mutiny silently waiting to erupt.
Oblivious, she laughed for me and said
"Ee, luv, I'm th' appiest girl in th' world!"
I was glad it was true.

And there I stood in my white coat and blue trousers,
Wanting to be a friend rather than an Efficiency –
I didn't want to Organise her.
How I wished I could banish her threat of pain
With pink carnations, or the sun, or a song,
As I watched her head with the old, old mist of hair around
And helped her climb the stairs towards home.

Beautiful, wonderful Mary!
(How my throat hurt as she patted my hand)
"What would I do without you?" she said, and laughed.
I tried to laugh too (if only from duty).
Only my white coat and blue trousers stopped me
From hugging her to me and crushing the cancer
And climbing each stair for her, taking her back
To her pink carnations.

She is the sun and a song and pink carnations.
She was the truth when she told me of luck and of fortune,
And of the happiest girl in the world.

Frances Clewlow

Grandad

Grandad's dead
And I'm sorry about that.

He'd a huge black overcoat.
He felt proud in it.
You could have hidden
A football crowd in it.
Far too big –
It was a lousy fit
But Grandad didn't
Mind a bit.
He wore it all winter
With a squashed black hat.

Now he's dead
And I'm sorry about that.

He'd got twelve stories.
I'd heard every one of them
Hundreds of times
But that was the fun of them:
You knew what was coming
So you could join in.
He'd got big hands
And brown, grooved skin
And when he laughed
It knocked you flat.

Now he's dead
And I'm sorry about that.

Kit Wright

As I Was Going Down Treak Street

As I was going down Treak Street
For half a pound of treacle,
Who should I meet but my old friend Micky Thumps.
He said to me, "Wilt thou come to our wake?"
I thought a bit,
I thought a bit,
I said I didn't mind:
So I went.

As I was sitting on our doorstep
Who should come by but my old friend Micky Thumps' brother.
He said to me, "Wilt thou come to our house?
Micky is ill."
I thought a bit,
I thought a bit,
I said I didn't mind:
So I went.

And he were ill:
He were gradely ill.
He said to me,
"Wilt thou come to my funeral, mon, if I die?"
I thought a bit,
I thought a bit,
I said I didn't mind:
So I went.

And it *were* a funeral.
Some stamped on his grave:
Some spat on his grave:
But I scraped my eyes out for my old friend Micky Thumps.

Anon

A Child Said, "What is the grass?"

(from *Song of Myself*)

A child said, "What is the grass?" fetching it to me with full hands;
How could I answer the child? I do not know what it is, any more than he.

I guess it must be the flag of my disposition, out of hopeful green stuff woven.

Or I guess it is the handkerchief of the Lord,
A scented gift and remembrancer, designedly dropt,
Bearing the owner's name someway in the corner, that we may see and
    remark, and say, Whose?

Or I guess the grass is itself a child, the produced babe of the vegetation.

Or I guess it is a uniform hieroglyphic;
And it means, Sprouting alike in broad zones and narrow zones,
Growing among black folks as among white;
Kanuck, Tuckahoe, Congressman, Cuff, I give them the same, I receive them
    the same.

And now it seems to me the beautiful uncut hair of graves.

Tenderly will I use you, curling grass;
It may be you transpire from the breasts of young men;
It may be if I had known them I would have loved them;
It may be you are from old people, and from women, and from offspring
    taken soon out of their mothers' laps;
And here you are the mothers' laps.

This grass is very dark to be from the white heads of old mothers;
Darker than the colourless beards of old men;
Dark to come from under the faint red roofs of mouths.

O I perceive after all so many uttering tongues!
And I perceive they do not come from the roofs of mouths for nothing.

I wish I could translate the hints about the dead young men and women,
And the hints about old men and mothers, and the offspring taken soon out
  of their laps.

What do you think has become of the young and old men?
And what do you think has become of the women and children?

They are alive and well somewhere;
The smallest sprout shows there is really no death;
And if ever there was, it led forward life, and does not wait at the end to arrest
  it,
And ceas'd the moment life appear'd.

All goes onward and outward – nothing collapses;
And to die is different from what any one supposed, and luckier.

Has any one supposed it lucky to be born?
I hasten to inform him or her, it is just as lucky to die, and I know it.

Walt Whitman

Fear No More the Heat o' the Sun

Fear no more the heat o' the sun,
  Nor the furious winter's rages;
Thou thy worldly task hast done,
  Home art gone, and ta'en thy wages;
Golden lads and girls all must,
As chimney-sweepers, come to dust.

Fear no more the frown o' the great,
  Thou art past the tyrant's stroke:
Care no more to clothe and eat;
  To thee the reed is as the oak;
The sceptre, learning, physic, must
All follow this, and come to dust.

Fear no more the lightning-flash,
  Nor the all-dreaded thunder-stone;
Fear not slander, censure rash;
  Thou hast finish'd joy and moan:
All lovers young, all lovers must
Consign to thee, and come to dust.

No exorciser harm thee!
Nor no witchcraft charm thee!
Ghost unlaid forbear thee!
Nothing ill come near thee!
Quiet consummation have;
And renowned be thy grave!

William Shakespeare

In Painswick Churchyard

"Is this where people are buried?
I will not let them bury you"

He picnics among tombs
– pours imaginary tea,
a yew tree his kitchen

"You will live with me in my house"

Oh could I believe the living and dead inhabit one house under
the sky and you my child run into your future for ever

Frances Horovitz

The Song of Wandering Aengus

I went out to the hazel wood,
Because a fire was in my head,
And cut and peeled a hazel wand,
And hooked a berry to a thread,
And when white moths were on the wing,
And moth-like stars were flickering out.
I dropped the berry in a stream
And caught a little silver trout.

When I had laid it on the floor
I went to blow the fire a-flame
But something rustled on the floor,
And someone called me by my name:

It had become a glimmering girl
With apple blossoms in her hair
Who called me by my name and ran
And faded through the brightening air.

Though I am old with wandering
Through hollow lands and hilly lands,
I will find out where she has gone,
And kiss her lips and take her hands;
And walk among long dappled grass,
And pluck till time and times are done,
The silver apples of the moon,
The golden apples of the sun.

W. B. Yeats

Requiem

Under the wide and starry sky
   Dig the grave and let me lie:
Glad did I live and gladly die,
   And I laid me down with a will.

This be the verse you grave for me:
Here he lies where he long'd to be;
Home is the sailor, home from sea,
   And the hunter home from the hill.

Robert Louis Stevenson

Yes

Last night I dreamt again of Adam returning
To the Garden's scented, bubbling cauldron.

Eve was beside him,
Their shadows were cut adrift
And the hum of bees was in their blood,

And the world was slow and good and all
The warm and yawning newness of their flesh
Was fixed for ever in the glow of "Yes".

Brian Patten

The Burning Desert and the Cool Orchard

Bad Times, Good Times
Food and Drink
War and Peace
Fun and Games

Centrifugalised in Finsbury Park

Hey I just had a go on one of them
things! Didn't notice it had a name,
but anyone could see what it was going to do to you –

something like a giant-size round biscuit-tin without a lid
made of wire-netting, and all around the inside,
niches, like for statues, 30 or so, like coffins, only
upright, and open of course with the kind of lattice –
with a padded red heart at head-height.

Paid 25p, got myself a niche, and stood and waited
with a little chain dangling across my hips,
until it was full, the gate shut, the music started
and the thing began to whirl.

It wasn't the stomach, it was what to do with the head:
no good looking down, but if you let your head back
it felt as if it was going to go on going back, or off –
a bit peculiar, shut my eyes to get through that.

And as it whirled, the whole thing turned on end,
more or less vertical – well, I'd seen that right from
the park gates and couldn't believe it, which was why –
and opening my eyes again then, just found myself
lying there – lying down face up, lying up face down
over the whole fairground!

And it didn't make you scream like the top of the Big
Wheel, but smile – look up and everyone else is standing there,
hanging there, smiling, look down and you might as well be a lazy
bird on the wind, though I did forget I could let go,

and the only strange feeling was,
every time you were on the down side hurtling up again,
you left the skin of your face behind for a second.
You know I've never dared try anything quite like that
before, and it was just very nice!

And when it slowed down and sank down, and all of us
were ordinary upright, and unhitched our little chains,
I only staggered a couple of times, disappearing
on ground level into the dark – and nobody was sick.

Libby Houston

Reggae Sounds

Shock-black bubble-doun-beat bouncing
rock-wise tumble-doun sound music;
foot-drop find drum, blood story,
bass history is a moving
                is a hurting black story.

Thunda from a bass drum sounding
lightening from a trumpet and a organ,
bass and rhythm and trumpet double-up,
team-up with drums for a deep doun searching.

Rhythm of a tropical electrical storm
(cooled doun to the pace of the struggle),
flame-rhythm of historically yearning
flame-rhythm of the time of turning,
measuring the time for bombs and for burning.

Slow drop. make stop. move forward.
dig doun to the root of the pain;
shape it into violence for the people,
they will know what to do, they will do it.

Shock-black bubble-doun-beat bouncing
rock-wise tumble-doun sound music;
foot-drop find drum, blood story,
bass history is a moving
                is a hurting black story.

Linton Kwesi Johnson

Where Poems Came From

They came, I supposed, from London.
Or from somewhere in England – Heaven,
most likely: wasn't God, after all, a bit
chalky – the grey suit and silver hair,
the underwear somewhat neglectful –
wasn't he the sort, in his spare time,
    to be spinning out rhymes
    on the prettiness of things?

Journeys they claimed –
    over hills and vales,
    through moonlit doors,
    down the last furlong
    from Ghent to Aix –
        but they reached us
too heavy for words with chalk-dust.
They were chalk-dust and the tired eye,
they were trembling knees when all went
speechless at the eager end of Friday.
They were paper and they were
    words, books of them
yellowed in the classroom cupboard –
the place that poems truly came from.

Yet truly they came,
behind my back they talked
to me, though I heard no words,
their coming was not to do
with words.
    It was in the laughter of dogs
    way across the snow. I could smell it
    in freshly painted rooms, taste it warmer
    in the cream than the milk. In the tricks
    that skies played with stone I found it,
    I found it in my body when first
    I discovered its emptying joy
    and wanted, afraid, to share it.

They came too in forgotten
things, in the thing wholly strange –
        that I recognised.
And one mart-day they came,
in a farmer's voice as he sat
drinking tea,
    explaining to himself, trying
    to explain the world to himself.

But not in the words of his explanation,
not from the names did they come.
    For there's a space
    in things, a gap between
    the words for it and a wave's
    movement, its infinite motion.

As I stood,
    a baby, at the sea's edge
    I began to wail – for no misery,
    no joy that I could name –
    lost, quite lost for words

to be facing there our world's great noise,
    to be facing there its silence.

Nigel Jenkins

Motherless Child

Sometimes I feel like a motherless child,
Sometimes I feel like a motherless child,
Sometimes I feel like a motherless child,
A long ways from home,
A long ways from home.

Sometimes I feel like I'm almost gone,
Sometimes I feel like I'm almost gone,
Sometimes I feel like I'm almost gone,
A long ways from home,
A long ways from home.

Sometimes I feel like a feather in the air,
Sometimes I feel like a feather in the air,
Sometimes I feel like a feather in the air,
And I spread my wings and I fly,

I spread my wings and I fly.

Anon

Lean Out of the Window

Lean out of the window,
Goldenhair,
I heard you singing
A merry air.

My book is closed,
I read no more,
Watching the fire dance
On the floor.

I have left my book:
I have left my room:
For I heard you singing
Through the gloom,

Singing and singing
A merry air.
Lean out of the window,
Goldenhair.

James Joyce

Hard Times Ain't Gone Nowhere

Peoples' raving 'bout hard times, tell me what it's all about.
Peoples' raving 'bout hard times, tell me what it's all about.
Hard times don't worry me, I was broke when they first started out.

Friends, it could be worser, you don't seem to understand.
Friends, it could be worser, you don't seem to understand.
Some is crying with a sack of gold under each arm and a loaf of
    bread in each hand.

Peoples' raving 'bout hard times, I don't know why they should.
Peoples' raving 'bout hard times, I don't know why they should.
If some people was like me, they didn't have no money when
    times were good.

Lonnie Johnson

Winter

When icicles hang by the wall,
   And Dick the shepherd blows his nail,
And Tom bears logs into the hall,
   And milk comes frozen home in pail,
When blood is nipp'd and ways be foul,
Then nightly sings the staring owl,
                Tu-who;
Tu-whit, tu-who – a merry note,
While greasy Joan doth keel the pot.

When all aloud the wind doth blow,
   And coughing drowns the parson's saw.
And birds sit brooding in the snow,
   And Marian's nose looks red and raw,
When roasted crabs hiss in the bowl,
Then nightly sings the staring owl,
                Tu-who;
Tu-whit, tu-who – a merry note,
While greasy Joan doth keel the pot.

William Shakespeare

The Warm and the Cold

Freezing dusk is closing
   Like a slow trap of steel
On trees and roads and hills and all
   That can no longer feel.
      But the carp is in its depth
         Like a planet in its heaven.
      And the badger in its bedding
         Like a loaf in the oven.
      And the butterfly in its mummy
         Like a viol in its case.
      And the owl in its feathers
         Like a doll in its lace.

Freezing dusk has tightened
   Like a nut screwed tight
On the starry aeroplane
   Of the soaring night.
      But the trout is in its hole
         Like a chuckle in a sleeper.
      The hare strays down the highway
         Like a root going deeper.
      The snail is dry in the outhouse
         Like a seed in a sunflower.
      The owl is pale on the gatepost
         Like a clock on its tower.

Moonlight freezes the shaggy world
   Like a mammoth of ice –
The past and the future
   Are the jaws of a steel vice.
      But the cod is in the tide-rip
         Like a key in a purse.

The deer are on the bare-blown hill
Like smiles on a nurse.
The flies are behind the plaster
Like the lost score of a jig.
Sparrows are in the ivy-clump
Like money in a pig.

Such a frost
The flimsy moon
Has lost her wits.

A star falls.

The sweating farmers
Turn in their sleep
Like oxen on spits.

Ted Hughes

To a Poor Old Woman

munching a plum on
the street a paper bag
of them in her hand

They taste good to her
They taste good
to her. They taste
good to her

You can see it by
the way she gives herself
to the one half
sucked out in her hand

Comforted
a solace of ripe plums
seeming to fill the air
They taste good to her

William Carlos Williams

Rotting Song

old green cheese
old green cheese
you'll never get another chance —

Green cheese sits in the airtight tin
wondering just how those mites got in,
crosses off the minutes to the sinking knife —
hasn't found out he's in prison for life

Cold meat sweats on the larder plate
a wet flesh target, doesn't have to wait,
in dive the black flies, drop their eggs —
drive him crazy those hairy legs

Dud plum squashed on the kitchen floor
can't see what he's been put there for,
knows he's going soft but he can't stir —
old age buries him deep in fur

Dud plum, cold meat, old green cheese
rot in your own time at your ease,
nobody minds, nobody cares —
moved out their lives and gone downstairs

Libby Houston

Greedyguts

I sat in the café and sipped at a Coke.
There sat down beside me a WHOPPING great bloke
Who sighed as he elbowed me into the wall:
"Your trouble, my boy, is your belly's too small!
Your bottom's too thin! Take a lesson from me:
I may not be nice, but I'm GREAT, you'll agree,
And I've lasted a lifetime by playing this hunch:
The bigger the breakfast, the larger the lunch!

The larger the lunch, then the huger the supper.
The deeper the teapot, the vaster the cupper.
The fatter the sausage, the fuller the tea.
The MORE on the table, the BETTER for ME!"

His elbows moved in and his elbows moved out,
His belly grew bigger, chins wobbled about,
As forkful by forkful and plate after plate,
He ate and he ate and he ate and he ATE!

I hardly could breathe, I was squashed out of shape,
So under the table I made my escape.

"Aha!" he rejoiced, "when it's put to the test,
The fellow who's fattest will come off the best!
Remember, my boy, when it comes to the crunch:
The bigger the breakfast, the larger the lunch!

The larger the lunch, then the huger the supper.
The deeper the teapot, the vaster the cupper.
The fatter the sausage, the fuller the tea.
The MORE on the table, the BETTER for ME!"

A lady came by who was scrubbing the floor
With a mop and a bucket. To even the score,
I lifted that bucket of water and said,
As I poured the whole lot of it over his head:

"*I've* found all my life, it's a pretty sure bet:
The FULLER the bucket, the WETTER you GET!"

Kit Wright

Figgie Hobbin

Nightingales' tongues, your majesty?
   Quails in aspic, cost a purse of money?
Oysters from the deep, raving sea?
   Grapes and Greek honey?
Beads of black caviare from the Caspian?
   Rock melon with corn on the cob in?
Take it all away! grumbled the old King of Cornwall.
   Bring me some figgie hobbin!

Devilled lobster, your majesty?
   Scots kail brose or broth?
Grilled mackerel with gooseberry sauce?
   Cider ice that melts in your mouth?
Pears filled with nut and date salad?
   Christmas pudding with a tanner or a bob in?
Take it all away! groused the old King of Cornwall.
   Bring me some figgie hobbin!

Amber jelly, your majesty?
   Passion fruit flummery?
Pineapple sherbet, milk punch or Pavlova cake,
   Sugary, summery?

79

Carpet-bag steak, blueberry grunt, cinnamon crescents?
   Spaghetti as fine as the thread on a bobbin?
Take it all away! grizzled the old King of Cornwall.
   Bring me some figgie hobbin!

So in from the kitchen came figgie hobbin,
   Shining and speckled with raisins sweet,
And though on the King of Cornwall's land
   The rain it fell and wind it beat,
As soon as a forkful of figgie hobbin
   Up to his lips he drew,
Over the palace a pure sun shone
   And the sky was blue.
THAT'S what I wanted! he smiled, his face
   Now as bright as the breast of the robin.
To cure the sickness of the heart, ah –
   Bring me some figgie hobbin!

Charles Causley

Porridge

Why is there no monument
   To Porridge in our land?
If it's good enough to eat
   It's good enough to stand!

On a plinth in London
   A statue we should see
Of Porridge made in Scotland
   Signed "Oatmeal, O.B.E."
       (By a young dog of three)

Spike Milligan

I Hear an Army Charging

I hear an army charging upon the land,
    And the thunder of horses plunging, foam about their knees:
Arrogant, in black armour, behind them stand,
    Disdaining the reins, with fluttering whips, the charioteers.

They cry unto the night their battle-name:
    I moan in sleep when I hear afar their whirling laughter.
They cleave the gloom of dreams, a blinding flame,
    Clanging, clanging upon the heart as upon an anvil.

They come shaking in triumph their long, green hair:
    They come out of the sea and run shouting by the shore.
My heart, have you no wisdom thus to despair?
    My love, my love, my love, why have you left me alone?

James Joyce

The Field of Waterloo

Yea, the coneys are scared by the thud of hoofs,
And their white scuts flash at their vanishing heels,
And swallows abandon the hamlet-roofs.

The mole's tunnelled chambers are crushed by wheels,
The lark's eggs scattered, their owners fled;
And the hedgehog's household the sapper unseals.

The snail draws in at the terrible tread,
But in vain; he is crushed by the felloe-rim;
The worm asks what can be overhead,

81

And wriggles deep from a scene so grim,
And guesses him safe; for he does not know
What a foul red flood will be soaking him!

Beaten about by the heel and toe
Are butterflies, sick of the day's long rheum,
To die of a worse than the weather-foe.

Trodden and bruised to a miry tomb
Are ears that have greened but will never be gold,
And flowers in the bud that will never bloom.

Thomas Hardy

Tommy

I went into a public-'ouse to get a pint o' beer,
The publican 'e up an' sez, "We serve no red-coats here."
The girls be'ind the bar they laughed an' giggled fit to die,
I outs into the street again an' to myself sez I:
    O it's Tommy this, an' Tommy that, an' "Tommy, go away";
    But it's "Thank you, Mister Atkins," when the band begins to play –
    The band begins to play, my boys, the band begins to play,
    O it's "Thank you, Mister Atkins," when the band begins to play.

I went into a theatre as sober as could be,
They gave a drunk civilian room, but 'adn't none for me;
They sent me to the gallery or round the music-'alls,
But when it comes to fightin', Lord! they'll shove me in the stalls!
    For it's Tommy this, an' Tommy that, an' "Tommy, wait outside";
    But it's "Special train for Atkins" when the trooper's on the tide –
    The troopship's on the tide, my boys, the troopship's on the tide,
    O it's "Special train for Atkins" when the trooper's on the tide.

Yes, makin' mock o' uniforms that guard you while you sleep
Is cheaper than them uniforms, an' they're starvation cheap;
An' hustlin' drunken soldiers when they're goin' large a bit
Is five times better business than paradin' in full kit.
    Then it's Tommy this, an' Tommy that, an' "Tommy, 'ow's yer soul?"
    But it's "Thin red line of 'eroes" when the drums begin to roll –
    The drums begin to roll, my boys, the drums begin to roll,
    O it's "Thin red line of 'eroes" when the drums begin to roll.

We aren't no thin red 'eroes, nor we aren't no blackguards too,
But single men in barricks, most remarkable like you;
An' if sometimes our conduck isn't all your fancy paints,
Why, single men in barricks don't grow into plaster saints;
    While it's Tommy this, an' Tommy that, an' "Tommy, fall be'ind,"
    But it's "Please to walk in front, sir," when there's trouble in the wind –
    There's trouble in the wind, my boys, there's trouble in the wind,
    O it's "Please to walk in front, sir," when there's trouble in the wind.

You talk o' better food for us, an' schools, an' fires, an' all:
We'll wait for extry rations if you treat us rational.
Don't mess about the cook-room slops, but prove it to our face
The Widow's Uniform is not the soldier-man's disgrace.
    For it's Tommy this, an' Tommy that, an' "Chuck him out, the brute!"
    But it's "Saviour of 'is country" when the guns begin to shoot;
    An' it's Tommy this, an' Tommy that, an' anything you please;
    An' Tommy ain't a bloomin' fool – you bet that Tommy sees!

Rudyard Kipling

THE ORCHARD BOOK OF POEMS

Johnny, I Hardly Knew Ye

While going the road to sweet Athy,
    Hurroo! hurroo!
While going the road to sweet Athy,
    Hurroo! hurroo!
While going the road to sweet Athy,
A stick in my hand and a drop in my eye,
A doleful damsel I heard cry –
    "Och, Johnny, I hardly knew ye!
With drums and guns and guns and drums,
    The enemy nearly slew ye,
    My darling dear, you look so queer,
    Och, Johnny, I hardly knew ye!

"Where are your eyes that looked so mild?
    Hurroo! hurroo!
Where are your eyes that looked so mild?
    Hurroo! hurroo!
Where are your eyes that looked so mild
When my poor heart you first beguiled?
Why did you run from me and the child?
    Och, Johnny, I hardly knew ye!
With drums and guns and guns and drums,
    The enemy nearly slew ye,
    My darling dear, you look so queer,
    Och, Johnny, I hardly knew ye!

"Where are the legs with which you run?
    Hurroo! hurroo!
Where are the legs with which you run?
    Hurroo! hurroo!
Where are the legs with which you run,
When you went to carry a gun?

Indeed, your dancing days are done!
    Och, Johnny, I hardly knew ye!
With drums and guns and guns and drums,
    The enemy nearly slew ye,
    My darling dear, you look so queer,
    Och, Johnny, I hardly knew ye!

"It grieved my heart to see you sail,
    Hurroo! hurroo!
It grieved my heart to see you sail,
    Hurroo! hurroo!
It grieved my heart to see you sail,
Though from my heart you took leg bail –
Like a cod you're doubled up head and tail.
    Och, Johnny, I hardly knew ye!
With drums and guns and guns and drums,
    The enemy nearly slew ye,
    My darling dear, you look so queer,
    Och, Johnny, I hardly knew ye!

"You haven't an arm and you haven't a leg,
    Hurroo! hurroo!
You haven't an arm and you haven't a leg,
    Hurroo! hurroo!
You haven't an arm and you haven't a leg,
You're an eyeless, noseless, chickenless egg;
You'll have to be put in a bowl to beg;
    Och, Johnny, I hardly knew ye!
With drums and guns and guns and drums,
    The enemy nearly slew ye,
    My darling dear, you look so queer,
    Och, Johnny, I hardly knew ye!

"I'm happy for to see you home,
　　Hurroo! hurroo!
I'm happy for to see you home,
　　Hurroo! hurroo!
I'm happy for to see you home,
All from the island of Sulloon,
So low in flesh, so high in bone,
　　Och, Johnny, I hardly knew ye!
With drums and guns and guns and drums,
　　The enemy nearly slew ye,
　　My darling dear, you look so queer,
　　Och, Johnny, I hardly knew ye!

"But sad as it is to see you so,
　　Hurroo! hurroo!
But sad as it is to see you so,
　　Hurroo! hurroo!
But sad as it is to see you so,
And to think of you now as an object of woe,
Your Peggy'll still keep ye on as her beau;
　　Och, Johnny, I hardly knew ye!
With drums and guns and guns and drums,
　　The enemy nearly slew ye,
　　My darling dear, you look so queer,
　　Och, Johnny, I hardly knew ye!"

Anon

How Much Longer?

Day after day after day it goes on
and no one knows how to stop it or escape.
Friends come bearing impersonal agonies,
I hear our hopeless laughter, I watch us drink.

War is in everyone's eyes, war is made
in the kitchen, in the bedroom, in the car at stoplights.
A marriage collapses like a burning house
and the other houses smoulder. Old friends
make their way in silence. Students stare
at their teachers, and suddenly feel afraid.
The old people are terrified like cattle
rolling their eyes and bellowing, while the young
wander in darkness, dazed, half-believing
some half-forgotten poem, or else come out
with their hearts on fire, alive in the last days.
Small children roam the neighbourhoods armed
with submachineguns, gas masks and riot sticks.
Excavations are made in us and slowly
we are filled in with used-up things: knives
too dull to cut bread with, bombs that failed to go off,
cats smashed on the highway, broken pencils,
slivers of soap, hair, gristle, old TV sets
that hum and stare out blindly like the insane.
Bridges kneel down, the cities billow and plunge
like horses in their smoke, the tall buildings
open their hysterical burning eyes at night,
the leafy suburbs look up at the clouds and tremble –
and my wife leaves her bed before dawn, walking
the icy pasture, shrieking her grief to the cows,
praying in tears to the softening blackness. I hear her
outside the window, crazed, inconsolable,
and go out to fetch her. Yesterday she saw
a photograph, Naomi our little girl
in a ditch in Viet Nam, half in the water,
the rest of her, beached on the mud, was horribly burned.

Robert Mezey

A Hard Rain's A-Gonna Fall

Oh, where have you been, my blue-eyed son?
Oh, where have you been, my darling young one?
I've stumbled on the side of twelve misty mountains,
I've walked and I've crawled on six crooked highways,
I've stepped in the middle of seven sad forests,
I've been out in front of a dozen dead oceans,
I've been ten thousand miles in the mouth of a graveyard,
And it's a hard, and it's a hard, it's a hard, and it's a hard,
And it's a hard rain's a-gonna fall.

Oh, what did you see, my blue-eyed son?
Oh, what did you see, my darling young one?
I saw a newborn baby with wild wolves all around it,
I saw a highway of diamonds with nobody on it,
I saw a black branch with blood that kept drippin',
I saw a room full of men with their hammers a-bleedin',
I saw a white ladder all covered with water,
I saw ten thousand talkers whose tongues were all broken,
I saw guns and sharp swords in the hands of young children,
And it's a hard, and it's a hard, it's a hard, it's a hard,
And it's a hard rain's a-gonna fall.

And what did you hear, my blue-eyed son?
And what did you hear, my darling young one?
I heard the sound of a thunder, it roared out a warnin',
Heard the roar of a wave that could drown the whole world,
Heard one hundred drummers whose hands were a-blazin',
Heard ten thousand whisperin' and nobody listenin',
Heard one person starve, I heard many people laughin',
Heard the song of a poet who died in the gutter,
Heard the sound of a clown who cried in the alley,
And it's a hard, and it's a hard, it's a hard, it's a hard,
And it's a hard rain's a-gonna fall.

Oh, who did you meet, my blue-eyed son?
Who did you meet, my darling young one?
I met a young child beside a dead pony,
I met a white man who walked a black dog,
I met a young woman whose body was burning,
I met a young girl, she gave me a rainbow,
I met one man who was wounded in love,
I met another man who was wounded with hatred,
And it's a hard, it's a hard, it's a hard, it's a hard,
It's a hard rain's a-gonna fall.

Oh, what'll you do now, my blue-eyed son?
Oh, what'll you do now, my darling young one?
I'm a-goin' back out 'fore the rain starts a-fallin',
I'll walk to the depths of the deepest black forest,
Where the people are many and their hands are all empty,
Where the pellets of poison are flooding their waters,
Where the home in the valley meets the damp dirty prison,
Where the executioner's face is always well hidden,
Where hunger is ugly, where souls are forgotten,
Where black is the colour, where none is the number,
And I'll tell it and think it and speak it and breathe it,
And reflect it from the mountain so all souls can see it,
Then I'll stand on the ocean until I start sinkin',
But I'll know my song well before I start singin',
And it's a hard, it's a hard, it's a hard, it's a hard,
It's a hard rain's a-gonna fall.

Bob Dylan

Starting to Make a Tree

First we carried out the faggot of steel stakes; they varied in
length, though most were taller than a man.

We slid one free of the bundle and drove it into the ground, first
padding the top with rag, that the branch might not be injured
with leaning on it.

Then we took turns to choose stakes of the length we wanted,
and to feel for the distances between them. We gathered to
thrust them firmly in.

There were twenty or thirty of them in all; and when they
were in place we had, round the clearing we had left for the
trunk, an irregular radial plantation of these props, each with
its wad of white at the tip. It was to be an old, downcurving tree.

This was in keeping with the burnt, chemical blue of the soil,
and the even hue of the sky which seemed to have been washed
with a pale brownish smoke;

another clue was the flatness of the horizon on all sides except
the north, where it was broken by the low slate or tarred
shingle roofs of the houses, which stretched away from us for
a mile or more.

This was the work of the morning. It was done with care, for
we had no wish to make revisions;

we were, nonetheless, a little excited, and hindered the women
at their cooking in our anxiety to know whose armpit and
whose groin would help us most in the modelling of the bole,
and the thrust of the boughs.

That done, we spent the early dusk of the afternoon gathering
materials from the nearest houses; and there was plenty:

a great flock mattress; two carved chairs; cement; chicken-
wire; tarpaulin, a smashed barrel; lead piping; leather of all
kinds; and many small things.

In the evening we sat late, and discussed how we could best
use them. Our tree was to be very beautiful.

Roy Fisher

Shalom Bomb

I want a bomb, my own private bomb, my shalom bomb.
I'll test it in the morning, when my son awakes,
hot and stretching, smelling beautiful from sleep. Boom! Boom!

Come my son dance naked in the room.
I'll test it on the landing and wake my neighbours,
the masons and the whores and the students who live downstairs.

Oh I must have a bomb and I'll throw open windows and
count down as I whizz around the living room,
on his bike, with him flying angels on my shoulder;
and my wife dancing in her dressing gown.
I want a happy family bomb, a do-it-yourself bomb,
I'll climb on the roof and ignite it there about noon.
My improved design will gong the world and we'll all eat lunch.

My pretty little bomb will play a daytime lullaby and
thank you bomb for now my son falls fast asleep.
My love come close, close the curtains, my lovely bomb, my darling.

My naughty bomb. Burst around us, burst between us, burst within us.

Light up the universe, then linger, linger
while the drone of the world recedes.

Shalom bomb

I want to explode the breasts of my wife.
and wake everyone,
to explode over playgrounds and parks, just as children
come from schools. I want a laughter bomb,
filled with sherbet fountains, licorice allsorts, chocolate kisses,
candy floss,
tinsel and streamers, balloons and fireworks, lucky bags,
bubbles and masks and false noses.

I want my bomb to sprinkle the earth with roses.
I want a one-man-band bomb. My own bomb.

My live long and die happy bomb. My die peacefully of old age bomb
in my own bed bomb.
My Om Mane Padme Aum Bomb, My Tiddly Om Pom Bomb.
My goodnight bomb, my sleeptight bomb,
my see you in the morning bomb.
I want my bomb, my own private bomb, my Shalom bomb.

Bernard Kops

The Lake Isle of Innisfree

I will arise and go now, and go to Innisfree,
And a small cabin build there, of clay and wattles made;
Nine bean rows will I have there, a hive for the honey bee,
    And live alone in the bee-loud glade.

And I shall have some peace there, for peace comes dropping slow,
Dropping from the veils of the morning to where the cricket sings;
There midnight's all a glimmer, and noon a purple glow,
    And evening full of the linnet's wings.

I will arise and go now, for always night and day
I hear lake water lapping with low sounds by the shore;
While I stand on the roadway, or on the pavements grey,
    I hear it in the deep heart's core.

W. B. Yeats

Freedom

This mountain standing in the sun.
Out of the light into the heat
out of the heat into the wind
out of the wind into the sun.
Out of the rock onto the snow
out of the shadow of the rock
onto the rock below the peak,
off the rock into shadow.
Freedom cannot be ended.
Out of the snow onto the grass
out of the grass onto the face
out of the grass onto the snow.

Freedom cannot be ended.
Out of the cold into the light
out of the heat into the snow
out of the snow onto the grass
and off the grass into the trees
among the trees in the shadow
out of the trees onto the rock.
This mountain standing in the sun.

Peter Levi

Galway Races

It's there you'll see confectioners with sugar sticks and dainties,
The lozenges and oranges, lemonade and the raisins;
The gingerbread and spices to accommodate the ladies,
And a bit crubeen for threepence to be picking while you're able.

It's there you'll see the gamblers, the thimbles and the garters,
And the sporting Wheel of Fortune with the four and twenty quarters.
There was others without scruple pelting wattles at poor Maggy,
And her father well contented and he looking at his daughter.

It's there you'll see the pipers and fiddlers competing,
And the nimble-footed dancers and they tripping on the daisies.
There was others crying segars and lights, and bills of all the races,
With the colour of the jockeys, the prize and horses' ages.

It's there you'd see the jockeys and they mounted on most stately,
The pink and blue, the red and green, the Emblem of our nation.
When the bell was rung for starting, the horses seemed impatient,
Though they never stood on ground, their speed was so amazing.

There was half a million people there of all denominations,
The Catholic, the Protestant, the Jew and Prespetarian.
There was yet no animosity, no matter what persuasion,
But *failte* and hospitality, inducing fresh acquaintance.

Anon

When I Went to the Circus

When I went to the circus that had pitched on the waste lot
it was full of uneasy people
frightened of the bare earth and the temporary canvas
and the smell of horses and other beasts
instead of merely the smell of man.

Monkeys rode rather grey and wizened
on curly plump piebald ponies
and the children uttered a little cry –
and dogs jumped through hoops and turned somersaults
and then the geese scuttled in a little flock
and round the ring they went to the sound of the whip
then doubled, and back, with a funny up-flutter of wings –
and the children suddenly shouted out.

Then came the hush again, like a hush of fear.

The tight-rope lady, pink and blonde and nude-looking, with a few gold spangles
footed cautiously out on the rope, turned prettily, spun round
bowed, and lifted her foot in her hand, smiled, swung her parasol
to another balance, tripped round, poised, and slowly sank
her handsome thighs down, down, till she slept her splendid body on the rope.
When she rose, tilting her parasol, and smiled at the cautious people
they cheered, but nervously.

The trapeze man, slim and beautiful and like a fish in the air
swung great curves through the upper space, and came down like a star
– And the people applauded, with hollow, frightened applause.

The elephants, huge and grey, loomed their curved bulk through the dusk
and sat up, taking strange postures, showing the pink soles of their feet
and curling their precious live trunks like ammonites
and moving always with soft slow precision
as when a great ship moves to anchor.
The people watched and wondered, and seemed to resent the mystery
        that lies in beasts.

Horses, gay horses, swirling round and plaiting
in a long line, their heads laid over each other's necks;
they were happy, they enjoyed it;
all the creatures seemed to enjoy the game
in the circus, with their circus people.

But the audience, compelled to wonder
compelled to admire the bright rhythms of moving bodies
compelled to see the delicate skill of flickering human bodies
flesh flamey and a little heroic, even in a tumbling clown,
they were not really happy.
There was no gushing response, as there is at the film.

When modern people see the carnal body dauntless and flickering gay
playing among the elements neatly, beyond competition
and displaying no personality,
modern people are depressed.

Modern people feel themselves at a disadvantage.
They know they have no bodies that could play among the elements.
They have only their personalities, that are best seen flat, on the film,
flat personalities in two dimensions, imponderable and touchless.

And they grudge the circus people the swooping gay weight of limbs
that flower in mere movement,
and they grudge them the immediate, physical understanding they have
    with their circus beasts,
and they grudge them their circus-life altogether.

Yet the strange, almost frightened shout of delight that comes now and then
    from the children
shows that the children vaguely know how cheated they are of their birthright
in the bright wild circus flesh.

D. H. Lawrence

Lord Beginner's Victory Calypso, Lord's Cricket Ground, 1950

Cricket, lovely cricket,
At Lord's where I saw it;
Cricket, lovely cricket,
At Lord's where I saw it;
Yardley tried his best
But Goddard won the Test.
They gave the crowd plenty fun;
Second Test and West Indies won.

Chorus: With those two little pals of mine
Ramadhin and Valentine.

The King was there well attired,
So they started with Rae and Stollmeyer;
Stolly was hitting balls around the boundary,
But Wardle stopped him at twenty.

Rae had confidence,
So he put up a strong defence;
He saw the King was waiting to see,
So he gave him a century.

Chorus: With those two little pals of mine
Ramadhin and Valentine.

West Indies first innings total was three-twenty-six
Just as usual.
When Bedser bowled Christiani
The whole thing collapsed quite easily,
England then went on,
And made one-hundred-fifty-one;
West Indies then had two-twenty lead,
And Goddard said, 'That's nice indeed.'

Chorus: With those two little pals of mine
Ramadhin and Valentine.

Yardley wasn't broken-hearted
When the second innings started;
Jenkins was like a target
Getting the first five into his basket.
But Gomez broke him down,
While Walcott licked them around;
He was not out for one-hundred and sixty-eight,
Leaving Yardley to contemplate.

Chorus: The bowling was super-fine
Ramadhin and Valentine.

West Indies was feeling homely,
Their audience had them happy.
When Washbrook's century had ended,
West Indies' voices all blended.
Hats went in the air.
They jumped and shouted without fear;
So at Lord's was the scenery
Bound to go down in history.

Chorus: After all was said and done,
Second Test and West Indies won!

Egbert Moore
(*'Lord Beginner'*)

The Dance

In Breughel's great picture, The Kermess,
the dancers go round, they go round and
around, the squeal and the blare and the
tweedle of bagpipes, a bugle and fiddles
tipping their bellies (round as the thick-
sided glasses whose wash they impound)
their hips and their bellies off balance
to turn them. Kicking and rolling about
the Fair Grounds, swinging their butts, those
shanks must be sound to bear up under such
rollicking measures, prance as they dance
in Breughel's great picture, The Kermess.

William Carlos Williams

Surfers

Couched in a recess from the wind I've seen
ravens fly back and forth to this cliff-ledge,
and watched the sea returning, and its sheen

turn bluebottle-blue flecked with indigo,
as though ink dropped into an abalone
accounted for that darkening. The flow

is rapid, and surf blazes across flats
burnished a hard gold by the wind, ribbed sand
planed level as a sheet of glass. In hats

and beach shorts, the surfing crowd congregate
beneath the sea wall, and out of the wind,
absorb the sun's fierce energies, the slate-

like textures of their bodies oiled to bear
both sea and sun. Up here I watch those birds
drop down through a blue crystal of sea air

and comb beached drifts of wrack dried by the heat
to fossil strands where flies fester. Each wave
asserts a resonance – a drumming beat

communicated to the group who tan,
awaiting a heavier lift of surf
to call them to their boards. I watch a man

squat down, his pulse picking up the rhythm
of each new smoking wall of surf that gains
momentum, shot through with light by the sun

to subside with a mulling poker's hiss.
He's like a sentry in his black peaked cap,
maintaining vigil, and at his raised fist

the word is out, and down the beach they race
these tiny figures running with their boards
into the wind and the blue rim of space.

Jeremy Reed

Seven Activities for a Young Child

Turn on the tap for straight and silver water in the sink,
Cross your finger through
The sleek thread falling

— *One.*

Spread white sandgrains on a tray,
And make clean furrows with a bent stick
To stare for a meaning

— *Two.*

Draw some clumsy birds on yellow paper,
Confronting each other and as if to fly
Over your scribbled hill

— *Three.*

Cut rapid holes into folded paper, look
At the unfolded patterns, look
through the unfolded pattern

— Four.

Walk on any square stone of the pavement,
Or on any crack between, as long
As it's with no one or with someone

— Five.

Throw up a ball to touch the truest brick
Of the red, brick wall,
Catch it with neat, cupped hand

— Six.

Make up in your head a path, and name it,
Name where it will lead you,
Walk towards where it will lead you

— Seven.

One, two, three, four, five, six, seven:
Take-up-the-rag-doll-quietly-and-sing-her-to-sleep.

Alan Brownjohn

The Valley of Animals

Birds and Beasts

I Think I Could Turn and Live with Animals

(from Song of Myself)

I think I could turn and live with animals, they are so placid and self-contained;
I stand and look at them long and long.
They do not sweat and whine about their condition;
They do not lie awake in the dark and weep for their sins;
They do not make me sick discussing their duty to God;
Not one is dissatisfied – not one is demented with the mania of owning things;
Not one kneels to another, nor to his kind that lived thousands of years ago;
Not one is respectable or industrious over the whole earth.

Walt Whitman

From 'Auguries of Innocence'

To see a World in a grain of sand,
And a Heaven in a wild flower,
Hold Infinity in the palm of your hand,
And Eternity in an hour.

A robin redbreast in a cage
Puts all Heaven in a rage.
A dove-house fill'd with doves and pigeons
Shudders Hell thro' all its regions.
A dog starv'd at his master's gate
Predicts the ruin of the State.
A horse misus'd upon the road
Calls to Heaven for human blood.
Each outcry of the hunted hare
A fibre from the brain does tear.
A skylark wounded in the wing,
A cherubim does cease to sing.
The game-cock clipt and arm'd for fight
Does the rising sun affright.
Every wolf's and lion's howl
Raises from Hell a Human soul.
The wild deer, wandering here and there,
Keeps the Human soul from care.
The lamb misus'd breeds public strife,
And yet forgives the butcher's knife.
The bat that flits at close of eve
Has left the brain that won't believe.
The owl that calls upon the night
Speaks the unbeliever's fright.
He who shall hurt the little wren
Shall never be belov'd by men.

He who the ox to wrath has mov'd
Shall never be by woman lov'd.
The wanton boy that kills the fly
Shall feel the spider's enmity.
He who torments the chafer's sprite
Weaves a bower in endless night.
The caterpillar on the leaf
Repeats to thee thy mother's grief.
Kill not the moth nor butterfly,
For the Last Judgement draweth nigh.
He who shall train the horse to war
Shall never pass the polar bar.
The beggar's dog and widow's cat,
Feed them, and thou wilt grow fat.

William Blake

Poem

As the cat
climbed over
the top of

the jamcloset
first the right
forefoot

carefully
then the hind
stepped down

into the pit of
the empty
flowerpot

William Carlos Williams

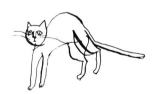

Skimbleshanks: the Railway Cat

There's a whisper down the line at 11.39
When the Night Mail's ready to depart,
Saying "Skimble where is Skimble has he gone to hunt the thimble?
We must find him or the train can't start."
All the guards and all the porters and the stationmaster's daughters
They are searching high and low,
Saying "Skimble where is Skimble for unless he's very nimble
Then the Night Mail just can't go."
At 11.42 then the signal's overdue
And the passengers are frantic to a man –
Then Skimble will appear and he'll saunter to the rear:
He's been busy in the luggage van!
    He gives one flash of his glass-green eyes
        And the signal goes "All Clear!"
    And we're off at last for the northern part
        Of the Northern Hemisphere!

You may say that by and large it is Skimble who's in charge
Of the Sleeping Car Express.
From the driver and the guards to the bagmen playing cards
He will supervise them all, more or less.
Down the corridor he paces and examines all the faces
Of the travellers in the First and in the Third;
He establishes control by a regular patrol
And he'd know at once if anything occurred.

He will watch you without winking and he sees what you are thinking
And it's certain that he doesn't approve
Of hilarity and riot, so the folk are very quiet
When Skimble is about and on the move.
    You can play no pranks with Skimbleshanks!
      He's a Cat that cannot be ignored;
    So nothing goes wrong on the Northern Mail
      When Skimbleshanks is aboard.

Oh it's very pleasant when you have found your little den
With your name written up on the door.
And the berth is very neat with a newly folded sheet
And there's not a speck of dust on the floor.
There is every sort of light – you can make it dark or bright:
There's a button that you turn to make a breeze.
There's a funny little basin you're supposed to wash your face in
And a crank to shut the window if you sneeze.
Then the guard looks in politely and will ask you very brightly
"Do you like your morning tea weak or strong?"
But Skimble's just behind him and was ready to remind him,
For Skimble won't let anything go wrong.
    And when you creep into your cosy berth
      And pull up the counterpane,
    You ought to reflect that it's very nice
    To know that you won't be bothered by mice –
    You can leave all that to the Railway Cat,
      The Cat of the Railway Train!

In the watches of the night he is always fresh and bright;

Every now and then he has a cup of tea

With perhaps a drop of Scotch while he's keeping on the watch,

Only stopping here and there to catch a flea.

You were fast asleep at Crewe and so you never knew

That he was walking up and down the station;

You were sleeping all the while he was busy at Carlisle,

Where he greets the stationmaster with elation.

But you saw him at Dumfries, where he summons the police

If there's anything they ought to know about:

When you get to Gallowgate there you do not have to wait –

For Skimbleshanks will help you to get out!

    He gives you a wave of his long brown tail

        Which says: "I'll see you again!

    You'll meet without fail on the Midnight Mail

        The Cat of the Railway Train."

T. S Eliot

A Dog in San Francisco

Sitting in an empty house

with a dog from the Mexican Circus!

O Daisy, embrace is my only pleasure.

Holding and hugging my friends. Education.

A wave of eucalyptus. Warm granite.
These are the things I have in my heart.
Heart and skills, there's nothing else.

I usually don't like small dogs but you
like midwestern women take over the air.
You leap into the air and pivot
a diver going up! You are known
to open the fridge and eat when you wish
you can roll down car windows and step out
you know when to get off the elevator.

I always wanted to be a dog
but I hesitated
for I thought they lacked certain skills.
Now I want to be a dog.

Michael Ondaatje

Today I Saw the Dragon-fly

Today I saw the dragon-fly
Come from the wells where he did lie.

An inner impulse rent the veil
Of his old husk: from head to tail
Came out clear plates of sapphire mail.

He dried his wings: like gauze they grew;
Through crofts and pastures wet with dew
A living flash of light, he flew.

Alfred, Lord Tennyson

Praise of a Collie

She was a small dog, neat and fluid –
Even her conversation was tiny:
She greeted you with *bow*, never *bow-wow*.

Her sons stood monumentally over her
But did what she told them. Each grew grizzled
Till it seemed he was his own mother's grandfather.

Once, gathering sheep on a showery day,
I remarked how dry she was. Pollóchan said, "Ah,
It would take a very accurate drop to hit Lassie."

She sailed in the dinghy like a proper sea-dog.
Where's a burn? – she's first on the other side.
She flowed through fences like a piece of black wind.

But suddenly she was old and sick and crippled . . .
I grieved for Pollóchan when he took her a stroll
And put his gun to the back of her head.

Norman MacCaig

Blackbird

Blackbird singing in the dead of night
Take these broken wings and learn to fly.
All your life
You were only waiting for this moment to arise.
Blackbird singing in the dead of night
Take these sunken eyes and learn to see.
All your life
You were only waiting for this moment to be free.

Blackbird fly, Blackbird fly
Into the light of the dark black night.
Blackbird fly, Blackbird fly
Into the light of the dark black night.
Blackbird singing in the dead of night
Take these broken wings and learn to fly.
All your life
You were only waiting for this moment to arise
You were only waiting for this moment to arise
You were only waiting for this moment to arise

John Lennon and Paul McCartney

Byron's Dog, Boatswain

When Lord Byron's favourite dog died, the poet had
a marble monument erected to his memory, with this inscription:

NEAR THIS SPOT
ARE DEPOSITED THE REMAINS OF ONE
WHO POSSESSED BEAUTY WITHOUT VANITY,
STRENGTH WITHOUT INSOLENCE,
COURAGE WITHOUT FEROCITY,
AND ALL THE VIRTUES OF MAN WITHOUT HIS VICES.
THIS PRAISE, WHICH WOULD BE UNMEANING
FLATTERY IF INSCRIBED OVER HUMAN ASHES,
IS BUT A JUST TRIBUTE TO THE MEMORY OF
BOATSWAIN, A DOG,
WHO WAS BORN AT NEWFOUNDLAND, MAY 1803,
AND DIED AT NEWSTEAD ABBEY, NOV. 18, 1808.

Lord Byron

Ode to a Nightingale

My heart aches, and a drowsy numbness pains
  My sense, as though of hemlock I had drunk,
Or emptied some dull opiate to the drains
  One minute past, and Lethe-wards had sunk:
'Tis not through envy of thy happy lot,
  But being too happy in thine happiness, –
    That thou, light-winged Dryad of the trees,
      In some melodious plot
  Of beechen green, and shadows numberless,
    Singest of summer in full-throated ease.

O, for a draught of vintage! that hath been
  Cool'd a long age in the deep-delved earth,
Tasting of Flora and the country green,
  Dance, and Provençal song, and sunburnt mirth!
O for a beaker full of the warm South,
  Full of the true, the blushful Hippocrene,
    With beaded bubbles winking at the brim,
      And purple-stained mouth;
  That I might drink, and leave the world unseen,
    And with thee fade away into the forest dim:

Fade far away, dissolve, and quite forget
  What thou among the leaves hast never known,
The weariness, the fever, and the fret
  Here, where men sit and hear each other groan;
Where palsy shakes a few, sad, last grey hairs,
  Where youth grows pale, and spectre-thin, and dies;
    Where but to think is to be full of sorrow
      And leaden-eyed despairs,
  Where Beauty cannot keep her lustrous eyes,
    Or new Love pine at them beyond to-morrow.

Away! away! for I will fly to thee,
  Not charioted by Bacchus and his pards,
But on the viewless wings of Poesy,
  Though the dull brain perplexes and retards:
Already with thee! tender is the night,
  And haply the Queen-Moon is on her throne,
    Cluster'd around by all her starry Fays;
      But here there is no light,
  Save what from heaven is with the breezes blown
    Through verdurous glooms and winding mossy ways.

I cannot see what flowers are at my feet,
  Nor what soft incense hangs upon the boughs,
But, in embalmed darkness, guess each sweet
  Wherewith the seasonable month endows
The grass, the thicket, and the fruit-tree wild;
  White hawthorn, and the pastoral eglantine;
    Fast fading violets cover'd up in leaves;
      And mid-May's eldest child,
  The coming musk-rose, full of dewy wine,
    The murmurous haunt of flies on summer eves.

Darkling I listen; and, for many a time
  I have been half in love with easeful Death,
Call'd him soft names in many a mused rhyme,
  To take into the air my quiet breath;
Now more than ever seems it rich to die,
  To cease upon the midnight with no pain,
    While thou art pouring forth thy soul abroad
      In such an ecstasy!
  Still wouldst thou sing, and I have ears in vain —
    To thy high requiem become a sod.

THE ORCHARD BOOK OF POEMS

Thou wast not born for death, immortal Bird!
No hungry generations tread thee down;
The voice I hear this passing night was heard
In ancient days by emperor and clown:
Perhaps the self-same song that found a path
Through the sad heart of Ruth, when, sick for home,
She stood in tears amid the alien corn;
The same that oft-times hath
Charm'd magic casements, opening on the foam
Of perilous seas, in faery lands forlorn.

Forlorn! the very word is like a bell
To toll me back from thee to my sole self!
Adieu! the fancy cannot cheat so well
As she is fam'd to do, deceiving elf.
Adieu! adieu! thy plaintive anthem fades
Past the near meadows, over the still stream,
Up the hill-side; and now 'tis buried deep
In the next valley-glades:
Was it a vision, or a waking dream?
Fled is that music: – Do I wake or sleep?

John Keats

Magpies

One for sorrow
Two for joy
Three for a girl
Four for a boy

Five for silver
Six for gold
Seven for all the joys untold.

Anon

The Common Cormorant

The common cormorant or shag
Lays eggs inside a paper bag
The reason you will see no doubt
It is to keep the lightning out.
But what these unobservant birds
Have never noticed is that herds
Of wandering bears may come with buns
And steal the bags to hold the crumbs.

Anon

The Eagle

He clasps the crag with crooked hands;
Close to the sun in lonely lands,
Ring'd with the azure world, he stands.

The wrinkled sea beneath him crawls;
He watches from his mountain walls,
And like a thunderbolt he falls.

Alfred, Lord Tennyson

Lizard

A lizard ran out on a rock and looked up, listening
no doubt to the sounding of the spheres.
And what a dandy fellow! the right toss of a chin for you
and swirl of a tail!

If men were as much men as lizards are lizards
they'd be worth looking at.

D. H. Lawrence

Don't Call Alligator Long-Mouth till You Cross River

Call alligator long-mouth
call alligator saw-mouth
call alligator pushy-mouth
call alligator scissors-mouth
call alligator raggedy-mouth
call alligator bumpy-bum
call alligator all dem rude word
but better wait
                    till you cross river.

John Agard

To a Mouse, On Turning Her Up in Her Nest, With the Plough, November 1785

WEE, sleekit, cow'rin', tim'rous beastie,
O, what a panic's in thy breastie!
Thou need na start awa sae hasty,
   Wi' bickering brattle! scamper
I wad be laith to rin an' chase thee,
   Wi' murd'ring pattle!

I'm truly sorry Man's dominion
Has broken Nature's social union,
An' justifies that ill opinion,
   Which makes thee startle
At me, thy poor, earth-born companion,
   An' fellow-mortal!

I doubt na, whyles, but thou may thieve;
What then? poor beastie, thou maun live!
A daimen icker in a thrave
   'S a sma' request:
I'll get a blessin' wi' the lave,
   An' never miss't!

Thy wee-bit housie, too, in ruin!
It's silly wa's the win's are strewin'!
An' naething, now, to big a new ane,
   O' foggage green!
An' bleak December's winds ensuin',
   Baith snell an' keen!

Thou saw the fields laid bare an' waste,
An' weary Winter comin' fast,
An' cozie heare, beneath the blast,

Thou thought to dwell,
Till, crash! the cruel coulter past
   Out thro' thy cell.

That wee-bit heap o' leaves an' stibble
Has cost thee mony a weary nibble!
Now thou's turn'd out, for a' thy trouble,
   But house or hald,
To thole the Winter's sleety dribble,
   An' cranreuch cauld!

But, Mousie, thou art no thy lane,
In proving foresight may be vain:
The best-laid schemes o' Mice an' Men
   Gang aft a-gley, ·
An' lea'e us nought but grief an' pain,
   For promis'd joy!

Still thou art blest, compar'd wi' me!
The present only toucheth thee:
But, och! I backward cast my e'e
   On prospects drear!
An' forward, tho' I canna see,
   I guess an' fear!

Robert Burns

*Laith means loath; a pattle is a plough-staff; whyles means
sometimes; a daimen icker in a thrave means an odd ear of corn;
the lave means the sheaves of corn; silly here means feeble;
big means to build; foggage is moss; baith snell means biting;
the coulter is a blade attached to the plough; stibble is
stubble; a hald is a holding; to thole means to endure; cranreuch
is hoar frost; no thy lane means not alone; a-gley means awry.*

121

After Prévert

We are going to see the rabbit,
We are going to see the rabbit.
Which rabbit, people say?
Which rabbit, ask the children?
Which rabbit?
The only rabbit,
The only rabbit in England,
Sitting behind a barbed-wire fence
Under the floodlights, neon lights,
Sodium lights,
Nibbling grass
On the only patch of grass
In England, in England
(Except the grass by the hoardings
Which doesn't count.)
We are going to see the rabbit
And we must be there on time.

First we shall go by escalator,
Then we shall go by underground,
And then we shall go by motorway
And then by helicopterway,
And the last ten yards we shall have to go
On foot.

And now we are going
All the way to see the rabbit,
We are nearly there,
We are longing to see it,
And so is the crowd

Which is here in thousands
With mounted policemen
And big loudspeakers
And bands and banners,
And everyone has come a long way.
But soon we shall see it
Sitting and nibbling
The blades of grass
On the only patch of grass
In – but something has gone wrong!
Why is everyone so angry,
Why is everyone jostling
And slanging and complaining?

The rabbit has gone,
Yes, the rabbit has gone.
He has actually burrowed down into the earth
And made himself a warren, under the earth,
Despite all these people.
And what shall we do?
What *can* we do?

It is all a pity, you must be disappointed,
Go home and do something else for today,
Go home again, go home for today.
For you cannot hear the rabbit, under the earth,
Remarking rather sadly to himself, by himself,
As he rests in his warren, under the earth:
"It won't be long, they are bound to come,
They are bound to come and find me, even here."

Alan Brownjohn

Epitaph on a Hare

Here lies, whom hound did ne'er pursue,
  Nor swifter greyhound follow,
Whose foot ne'er tainted morning dew,
  Nor ear heard huntsman's halloo,

Old Tiney, surliest of his kind,
  Who, nurs'd with tender care,
And to domestic bounds confin'd,
  Was still a wild Jack-hare.

Though duly from my hand he took
  His pittance ev'ry night,
He did it with a jealous look,
  And, when he could, would bite.

His diet was of wheaten bread,
  And milk, and oats, and straw;
Thistles, or lettuces instead,
  With sand to scour his maw.

On twigs of hawthorn he regal'd,
  On pippins' russet peel,
And, when his juicy salads fail'd,
  Slic'd carrot pleas'd him well.

A Turkey carpet was his lawn,
  Whereon he lov'd to bound,
To skip and gambol like a fawn,
  And swing his rump around.

His frisking was at ev'ning hours,
    For then he lost his fear,
But most before approaching show'rs,
    Or when a storm drew near.

Eight years and five round-rolling moons
    He thus saw steal away,
Dozing out all his idle noons,
    And ev'ry night at play.

I kept him for his humour's sake,
    For he would oft beguile
My heart of thoughts, that made it ache,
    And force me to a smile.

But now beneath his walnut shade
    He finds his long last home,
And waits in snug concealment laid,
    Till gentler Puss shall come.

He still more aged feels the shocks,
    From which no care can save,
And, partner once of Tiney's box,
    Must soon partake his grave.

William Cowper

The Badger

When midnight comes a host of dogs and men
Go out and track the badger to his den,
And put a sack within the hole and lie
Till the old grunting badger passes bye.
He comes and hears – they let the strongest loose.
The old fox hears the noise and drops the goose.
The poacher shoots and hurries from the cry,
And the old hare half-wounded buzzes bye.
They get a forked stick to bear him down
And clap the dogs and take him to the town,
And bait him all the day with many dogs,
And laugh and shout and fright the scampering hogs.
He runs along and bites at all he meets;
They shout and hollo down the noisy streets.
He turns about to face the loud uproar
And drives the rebels to their very door.
The frequent stone is hurled where e'er they go;
When badgers fight, then everyone's a foe.
The dogs are clapt and urged to join the fray;
The badger turns and drives them all away.
Though scarcely half as big, demure and small,
He fights with dogs for bones and beats them all.
The heavy mastiff, savage in the fray,
Lies down and licks his feet and turns away.
The bulldog knows his match and waxes cold,
The badger grins and never leaves his hold.
He drives the crowd and follows at their heels
And bites them through – the drunkard swears and reels.

The frightened women take the boys away,
The blackguard laughs and hurries on the fray.
He tries to reach the woods, an awkward race,
But sticks and cudgels quickly stop the chase.
He turns agen and drives the noisy crowd
And beats the many dogs in noises loud.
He drives away and beats them every one,
And then they loose them all and set them on,
He falls as dead and kicked by boys and men,
Then starts and grins and drives the crowd agen;
Till kicked and torn and beaten out he lies
And leaves his hold and cackles, groans, and dies.

John Clare

Maninagar Days

They are always there
just as pigeons or flies
can be *always there*
and the children have to fight them off,
especially during those hot May afternoons
when they dare to jump down from the trees
into the cool shaded spots, the corners between
the canna flower beds
still moist from the mornings watering.

Monkeys in the garden –
I'm talking about rhesus monkeys
the colour of dirt roads and khaki
        and sometimes even of honey.
Rhesus monkeys that travel in small groups,
extended families; constantly feuding brothers, sisters,
uncles, aunts, cousins screaming through
the trees – while the grandmother sits farther away
sadly, holding on to the sleepy newborn.
Somehow they manage to make peace
before every meal.

Now and then a solitary langur:
the Hanuman-monkey, crossing the terrace
with the importance of someone going to the airport.
A lanky dancer's steps
with black hands, black feet
sharp as black leather gloves and black leather shoes
against the soft grey body.
Sharp
and yet delicate
as if they were brush-stroked in
with a Japanese flourish.
And black-faced too,
with thick tufts of silver grey eyebrows,
a bushy chin. So aloof
he couldn't be bothered
with anyone.

Some people live with rhesus monkeys
and langurs in their gardens.
To these children
the monkeys are as normal and common as dogs.
And yet, the monkeys remain magical.

The children feel closer
to the monkeys, although they never
really play together, although the monkeys
probably hate the children:
those three children, two girls and a boy
who are all a bit afraid
of the full-grown-to-their-prime males
that stretch themselves and stretch themselves
to the height of wisdom and fatherly wit.

The monkeys are not at all cuddly like toys.
No.
They are lean twirls, strong tails, fast shadows
abrupt with yellow teeth.
The monkeys are not so innocent
the elders warn,
not so content with their daily routine
for they are turning
into urban thieves, imitating
and even outdoing the crows:

One day a tall monkey leaped down on the clothesline
and stole a blinding white shirt.
Another day, a very muscular monkey
bounded out of the neighbour's house
with a huge rock of golden *gur*, solid raw sugar.
The boy was impressed. His mother
would have difficulty carrying such a load.
Still, the children treat the monkeys
as if they were children newly arrived from a foreign
country, unable to speak the language yet.

And the children's grandmother comes out
to the front door from time to time.
Just awakened from her afternoon nap, now
she readjusts her thin white sari
readjusts her thin white sari
and squints against the sun
watching over them all –
And the faint May breeze that struggles
through the monkey crowded branches
is Hanuman's breath.
How could you know it, how could you miss it
unless you had lived
in such a garden.

Monkeys in the garden.
They are always there,
usually in the gulmuhore trees
chewing on the sour rubbery leaves
and the even more delicious bright
scarlet-orange flowers: petals
sparkling as sliced blood oranges,
water-plump green stems . . .

The monkeys have become everything
to the children, although
the children are not aware of it yet,
and one summer the children can't help
learning everything from them:
their noise, their shadows, their defiant stare,
the way they shake their heads,
the curve of their elbows
their weight on the trees . . .
In fact, without the monkeys
the trees begin to look a little barren
to the children.

Oh there are days when the monkeys refuse
to come down from the gulmuhore trees
and that makes the children jealous
and unhappy.
Oh there are days when the monkeys
never intrude, never interfere
with the children's favourite hide-outs.
Peaceful days, one would think
with the monkeys chatter-reclining and nibbling,
dozing and basking, jabbering and
lice-picking safe above in the gulmuhore trees
while the children run about exhausting
one game after another right below.
Peaceful hours one would think.
But the children are jealous
for they too love to eat
the gulmuhore flowers and leaves.

Invariably they try
to convince the monkeys to throw some flowers down
and then, that failing,
invariably they try to persuade the monkeys
to come down into their garden
(maybe with some flowers)
and then, that failing,
they are simply angry, so angry
at the monkeys, they terrify them off
into the neighbouring gardens.

Oh with monkeys like that
the children believe in Hanuman.
In their secret wishes the children reinvent
the perfect monkey: Hanuman,
wild and fierce and loyal and gentle . . .

One day the boy defended his sisters
single-handedly with a stick like a sword
he chased the whole band of monkeys
not up the trees but to the back of the house:
a complete disappearance.
Then there was such silence
the girls were afraid – where
had all the birds gone? And the neighbour's dog?
A few minutes later the boy returned
running, chased by the monkeys,
and the stick like a sword was in the hand
of the angry leader . . .

Monkeys in the garden.
Some people have monkeys
in their dreams, monkeys in their nightmares,
monkeys crossing their shadows
long after they have stopped being children
long after they have left such a garden.

Sujata Bhatt

A Small Dragon

I've found a small dragon in the woodshed.
Think it must have come from deep inside a forest
because it's damp and green and leaves
are still reflecting in its eyes.

I fed it on many things, tried grass,
the roots of stars, hazel-nut and dandelion,
but it stared up at me as if to say, I need
foods you can't provide.

It made a nest among the coal,
not unlike a bird's but larger,
it is out of place here
and is quite silent.

If you believed in it I would come
hurrying to your house to let you share my wonder,
but I want instead to see
if you yourself will pass this way.

Brian Patten

Cow

The Cow comes home swinging
Her udder and singing:

"The dirt O the dirt
It does me no hurt.

And a good splash of muck
Is a blessing of luck.

O I splosh through the mud
But the breath of my cud

Is sweeter than silk.
O I splush through manure

But my heart stays as pure
As a pitcher of milk."

Ted Hughes

Blind Horse

He snuffles towards
pouches of water in the grass
and doesn't drink
when he finds them.

He twitches listlessly
at sappy grass stems and stands
stone still, his hanging head
caricatured with a scribble
of green whiskers.

134

Sometimes that head swings high,
ears cock – and he stares
down a long sound,
he stares and whinnies
for what never comes.

His eyes never close,
not in the heat of the day
when his leather lip droops and
he wears blinkers of flies.

At any time of the night
you hear him in his dark field
stamp the ground, stamp
the world down, waiting impatiently
for the light to break.

Norman MacCaig

The Lion

Strange spirit with inky hair,
   Tail tufted stiff in rage,
I saw with sudden stare
   Leap on the printed page.

The stillness of its roar
   From midnight deserts torn
Clove silence to the core
   Like the blare of a great horn.

I saw the sudden sky;
    Cities in crumbling sand;
The stars fall wheeling by;
    The lion roaring stand:

The stars fall wheeling by,
    Their silent, silver stain,
Cold on his glittering eye,
    Cold on his carven mane.

The full-orbed Moon shone down,
    The silence was so loud,
From jaws wide-open thrown
    His voice hung like a cloud.

Earth shrank to blackest air;
    That spirit stiff in rage
Into some midnight lair
    Leapt from the printed page.

W. J. Turner

The Lion and Albert

There's a famous seaside place called Blackpool,
    That's noted for fresh air and fun,
And Mr and Mrs Ramsbottom
    Went there with young Albert, their son.

A grand little lad was young Albert,
    All dressed in his best; quite a swell
With a stick with an 'orse's 'ead 'andle,
    The finest that Woolworth's could sell.

They didn't think much to the Ocean:
    The waves, they was fiddlin' and small,
There was no wrecks and nobody drownded,
    Fact, nothing to laugh at at all.

So, seeking for further amusement,
    They paid and went into the Zoo,
Where they'd Lions and Tigers and Camels,
    And old ale and sandwiches too.

There were one great big Lion called Wallace;
    His nose were all coverd with scars –
He lay in a somnolent posture
    With the side of his face on the bars.

Now Albert had heard about Lions,
    How they was ferocious and wild –
To see Wallace lying so peaceful,
    Well, it didn't seem right to the child.

So straightway the brave little feller,
    Not showing a morsel of fear,
Took his stick with its 'orse's 'ead 'andle
    And poked it in Wallace's ear.

You could see that the Lion didn't like it,
    For giving a kind of a roll,
He pulled Albert inside the cage with 'im,
    And swallowed the little lad 'ole.

Then Pa, who had seen the occurrence,
    And didn't know what to do next,
Said "Mother! Yon Lion's 'et Albert,"
    And Mother said "Well, I am vexed!"

Then Mr and Mrs Ramsbottom –
   Quite rightly, when all's said and done –
Complained to the Animal Keeper
   That the Lion had eaten their son.

The keeper was quite nice about it;
   He said "What a nasty mishap.
Are you sure that it's *your* boy he's eaten?"
   Pa said "Am I sure? There's his cap!"

The manager had to be sent for.
   He came and he said "What's to do?"
Pa said "Yon Lion's 'et Albert,
   And 'im in his Sunday clothes, too."

Then Mother said, "Right's right, young feller;
   I think it's a shame and a sin
For a lion to go and eat Albert,
   And after we've paid to come in."

The manager wanted no trouble,
   He took out his purse right away,
Saying "How much to settle the matter?"
   And Pa said "What do you usually pay?"

But Mother had turned a bit awkward
   When she thought where her Albert had gone.
She said "No! someone's got to be summonsed" –
   So that was decided upon.

Then off they went to the P'lice Station,
   In front of the Magistrate chap;
They told 'im what happened to Albert,
   And proved it by showing his cap.

The Magistrate gave his opinion
    That no one was really to blame
And he said that he hoped the Ramsbottoms
    Would have further sons to their name.

At that Mother got proper blazing,
    "And thank you, sir, kindly," said she.
"What, waste all our lives raising children
    To feed ruddy Lions? Not me!"

Marriott Edgar

The Kraken

Below the thunders of the upper deep;
Far, far beneath in the abysmal sea,
His ancient, dreamless, uninvaded sleep
The Kraken sleepeth: faintest sunlights flee
About his shadowy sides: above him swell
Huge sponges of millennial growth and height;
And far away into the sickly light,
From many a wondrous grot and secret cell
Unnumber'd and enormous polypi
Winnow with giant arms the slumbering green.
There hath he lain for ages and will lie
Battening upon huge seaworms in his sleep,
Until the latter fire shall heat the deep;
Then once by man and angels to be seen,
In roaring he shall rise and on the surface die.

Alfred, Lord Tennyson

The Lamb

Little Lamb who made thee
Dost thou know who made thee
Gave thee life & bid thee feed,
By the stream & o'er the mead;
Gave thee clothing of delight,
Softest clothing wooly bright;
Gave thee such a tender voice,
Making all the vales rejoice:
Little Lamb who made thee
Dost thou know who made thee

Little Lamb I'll tell thee,
Little Lamb I'll tell thee;
He is called by thy name,
For he calls himself a Lamb:
He is meek & he is mild,
He became a little child:
I a child & thou a lamb,
We are called by his name.
Little Lamb God bless thee,
Little Lamb God bless thee.

William Blake

The Tyger

Tyger Tyger, burning bright,
In the forests of the night;
What immortal hand or eye,
Could frame thy fearful symmetry?

In what distant deeps or skies,
Burnt the fire of thine eyes?
On what wings dare he aspire?
What the hand, dare sieze the fire?

And what shoulder, and what art,
Could twist the sinews of thy heart?
And when thy heart began to beat,
What dread hand? and what dread feet?

What the hammer? what the chain,
In what furnace was thy brain?
What the anvil? what dread grasp,
Dare its deadly terrors clasp?

When the stars threw down their spears
And water'd heaven with their tears:
Did he smile his work to see?
Did he who made the Lamb make thee?

Tyger Tyger burning bright,
In the forests of the night:
What immortal hand or eye,
Dare frame thy fearful symmetry?

William Blake

Caring for Animals

I ask sometimes why these small animals
With bitter eyes, why we should care for them.

I question the sky, the serene blue water,
But it cannot say. It gives no answer.

And no answer releases in my head
A procession of grey shades patched and whimpering,

Dogs with clipped ears, wheezing cart horses
A fly without shadow and without thought.

Is it with these menaces to our vision
With this procession led by a man carrying wood

We must be concerned? The holy land, the rearing
Green island should be kindlier than this.

Yet the animals, our ghosts, need tending to.
Take in the whipped cat and the blinded owl;

Take up the man-trapped squirrel upon your shoulder.
Attend to the unnecessary beasts.

From growing mercy and a moderate love
Great love for the human animal occurs.

And your love grows. Your great love grows and grows.

Jon Silkin

The Dazzling City

Work and Machinery
Towns and Cities

Sparkles from the Wheel

Where the city's ceaseless crowd moves on, the live-long day,
Withdrawn, I join a group of children watching – I pause aside with them.

By the kerb, toward the edge of the flagging,
A knife-grinder works at his wheel, sharpening a great knife;
Bending over, he carefully holds it to the stone – by foot and knee,
With measured tread, he turns rapidly – As he presses with light but firm hand,
Forth issue, then, in copious golden jets,
Sparkles from the wheel.

The scene, and all its belongings – how they seize and affect me!
The sad, sharp-chinned old man, with worn clothes, and broad shoulder band of leather;
Myself, effusing and fluid – a phantom curiously floating – now here absorb'd and arrested;

The group (an unminded point, set in a vast surrounding);
The attentive, quiet children – the loud, proud, restive base of the streets;
The low, hoarse purr of the whirling stone – the light-press'd blade,
Diffusing, dropping, sideways-darting, in tiny showers of gold,
Sparkles from the wheel.

Walt Whitman

The Sand Artist

On the damp seashore
above dark rainbows of shells, seaweed, seacoal,
the sandman wanders, seeking for a pitch.

Ebb tide is his time. The sands are lonely,
but a few lost families
camp for the day on its Easter emptiness.

He seeks the firm dark sand of the retreating waves.
– With their sandwiches and flasks of tea, they
lay their towels on the dry slopes of dunes.

From the sea's edge he draws his pail
of bitter brine, and bears it carefully
towards the place of first creation.

There he begins his labours. Silent,
not looking up at passing shadows
of curious children, he moulds his dreams.

Not simple sandcastles, melting as they dry,
but galleons, anchors, dolphins, cornucopias of fish,
mermaids, Neptunes, dragons of the deep.

With a piece of stick, a playing card
and the blunt fingers of a working man
the artist resurrects existence from the sea.

And as the returning tide takes back its gifts,
he waits in silence by his pitman's cap
for pennies from the sky.

James Kirkup

Big Wind

Where were the greenhouses going,
Lunging into the lashing
Wind driving water
So far down the river
All the faucets stopped? –
So we drained the manure-machine
For the steam plant,
Pumping the stale mixture
Into the rusty boilers,
Watching the pressure gauge
Waver over to red,
As the seams hissed
And the live steam
Drove to the far
End of the rose-house,
Where the worst wind was,
Creaking the cypress window-frames,
Cracking so much thin glass
We stayed all night,
Stuffing the holes with burlap;
But she rode it out,
That old rose-house,
She hove into the teeth of it,
The core and pith of that ugly storm,
Ploughing with her stiff prow,
Bucking into the wind-waves
That broke over the whole of her,
Flailing her sides with spray,
Flinging long strings of wet across the roof-top,
Finally veering, wearing themselves out, merely

Whistling thinly under the wind-vents;
She sailed until the calm morning,
Carrying her full cargo of roses.

Theodore Roethke

Song: Lift-Boy

Let me tell you the story of how I began:
I began as the boot-boy and ended as the boot-man,
With nothing in my pockets but a jack-knife and a button,
With nothing in my pockets but a jack-knife and a button,
With nothing in my pockets.

Let me tell you the story of how I went on:
I began as the lift-boy and ended as the lift-man,
With nothing in my pockets but a jack-knife and a button,
With nothing in my pockets but a jack-knife and a button,
With nothing in my pockets.

I found it very easy to whistle and play
With nothing in my head or my pockets all day,
With nothing in my pockets.

But along came Old Eagle, like Moses or David,
He stopped at the fourth floor and preached me Damnation:
"Not a soul shall be savèd, not one shall be savèd.
The whole First Creation shall forfeit salvation:
From knife-boy to lift-boy, from ragged to regal,
Not one shall be savèd, not you, not Old Eagle,
No soul on earth escapeth, even if all repent –"
So I cut the cords of the lift and down we went,
With nothing in our pockets.

Robert Graves   **147**

Go to Ahmedabad

Go walk the streets of Baroda,
go to Ahmedabad,
go breathe the dust
until you choke and get sick
with a fever no doctor's heard of.
Don't ask me
for I will tell you nothing
about hunger and suffering.

As a girl I learned
never to turn anyone away
from our door. Ma told me
give fresh water, good food,
nothing you wouldn't eat.
Hunger is when your mother
tells you years later
in America the doctor says
she is malnourished,
her bones are weak
because there was never enough
food for the children,
hers and the women who came
to our door with theirs.
The children must always be fed.
Hunger is when your mother is sick
in America because she wanted you
to eat well. Hunger is
when you walk
down the streets of Ahmedabad
and instead of handing out
coins to everyone
you give them tomatoes, cucumbers,

and go home with your mouth
tasting of burnt eucalyptus leaves
because you've lost
your appetite.
And yet, I say nothing
about hunger, nothing.

I have friends everywhere.
This time we met after ten years.
Someone died.
Someone got married.
Someone just had a baby.
And I hold the baby
because he's crying,
because there's a strange rash
all over his chest.
And my friend says
do you have a child? Why not?
When will you get married?
And the bus arrives
crowded with people hanging
out the doors and windows.
And her baby cries
in my arms, cries
so an old man wakes up and yells
at me: How could I let
my child get so sick?
Luckily, just then
someone tells a good joke.

I have friends everywhere.
This time we met after ten years.
And suffering is
when I walk around Ahmedabad
for this is the place

149

I always loved
this is the place
I always hated
for this is the place
I can never be at home in
this is the place
I will always be at home in.
Suffering is
When I'm in Ahmedabad
after ten years
and I learn for the first time
I will never choose
to live here. Suffering is
living in America
and not being able
to write a damn thing
about it. Suffering is
not for me to tell you about.

Go walk the streets of Baroda,
go to Ahmedabad
and step around the cow-dung
but don't forget
to look at the sky.
It's special in January,
you'll never see kites like these again.
Go meet the people if you can
and if you want to know
about hunger, about suffering,
go live it for yourself.
When there's an epidemic,
when the doctor says
your brother may die soon,
your father may die soon –

don't ask me how it feels.
It does not feel good.
That's why we make
tea with tulsi leaves,
that's why there's always someone
who knows a good story.

Sujata Bhatt

If I Were Walking

If I were walking along the canal
I would look in at me reading by the window
and think – I wish I was reading
by that window overlooking the canal
instead of walking along here by the canal
in the rain
and I would look in at all the other windows
and see the pictures on their walls
and the televisions they talk to
and perhaps even the different kinds of tea
moving from hand to hand
each in his own kind of room
and I would feel the damp
rise from the green leaves
where it had just sunk
and all along the walls
the leaves would die an inch more tonight
if I were walking there
looking in at me.

Michael Rosen

White Child Meets Black Man

She caught me outside a London
suburban shop, I like a giraffe
and she a mouse. I tried to go
but felt she stood
lovely as light on my back.

I turned with hello
and waited. Her eyes got
wider but not her lips.
Hello I smiled again and watched.

She stepped around me
slowly, in a kind of dance,
her wide eyes searching
inch by inch up and down:
no fur no scales no feathers
no shell. Just a live silhouette,
wild and strange
and compulsive
till mother came horrified.

"Mummy is his tummy black?"
Mother grasped her and swung
toward the crowd. She tangled
mother's legs looking back at me.
As I watched them birds were singing.

James Berry

Comprehensive

Tutumantu is like hopscotch, Kwani-kwani is
    like hide-and-seek.
When my sister came back to Africa she could
    only speak
English. Sometimes we fought in bed because
    she didn't know
what I was saying. I like Africa better than
    England.
My mother says You will like it when we get
    our own house.
We talk a lot about the things we used to do
in Africa and then we are happy.

Wayne. Fourteen. Games are for kids. I support
the National Front. Paki-bashing and pulling
    girls'
knickers down. Dad's got his own mini-cab.
    We watch
the video. I Spit on Your Grave. Brilliant.
I don't suppose I'll get a job. It's all them
coming over here to work. Arsenal.

Masjid at 6 o'clock. School at 8. There was
a friendly shop selling flour. They kneaded
    it at home
to make the evening nan. Families face Mecca.
There was much more room to play than here
    in London.
We played in an old village. It is empty now.
We got a plane to Heathrow. People wrote to us
that everything was easy here.

It's boring. Get engaged. Probably work in
    Safeways
worst luck. I haven't lost it yet because I want
respect. Marlon Frederic's nice but he's a bit dark.
I like Madness. The lead singer's dead good.
My mum is bad with her nerves. She won't
let me do nothing. Michelle. It's just boring.

Ejaz. They put some sausages on my plate.
As I was going to put one in my mouth
a Moslem boy jumped on me and pulled.
The plate dropped on the floor and broke. He
    asked me in Urdu
if I was a Moslem. I said Yes. You shouldn't
    be eating this.
It's a pig's meat. So we became friends.

My sister went out with one. There was murder.
I'd like to be mates, but they're different from us.
Some of them wear turbans in class. You can't
    help
taking the piss. I'm going in the Army.
No choice really. When I get married
I might emigrate. A girl who can cook
with long legs. Australia sounds all right.

Some of my family are named after the Moghul
    emperors.
Aurangzeb, Jehangir, Babur, Humayun. I was
    born
thirteen years ago in Jhelum. This is a hard
    school.

A man came in with a milk crate. The teacher
  told us
to drink our milk. I didn't understand what
  she was saying,
so I didn't go to get any milk. I have hope
  and am ambitious.
At first I felt as if I was dreaming, but I wasn't.
Everything I saw was true.

Carol Ann Duffy

Casey Jones

Come, all you rounders, if you want to hear
A story 'bout a brave engineer.
Casey Jones was the rounder's name
On a six-eight wheeler, boys, he won his fame.
The caller called Casey at a half past four,
Kissed his wife at the station door,
Mounted to the cabin with his orders in his hand
And he took his farewell trip to the promised land:
  Casey Jones, mounted to the cabin,
  Casey Jones, with his orders in his hand,
  Casey Jones, mounted to the cabin,
  And he took his farewell trip to the promised land.

"Put in your water and shovel in your coal,
Put your head out the window, watch them drivers roll,
I'll run her till she leaves the rail
'Cause I'm eight hours late with the western mail."
He looked at his watch and his watch was slow,
He looked at the water and the water was low,
He turned to the fireman and then he said,
"We're goin' to reach Frisco but we'll all be dead":

Casey Jones, goin' to reach Frisco,
Casey Jones, but we'll all be dead,
Casey Jones, goin' to reach Frisco,
"We're goin' to reach Frisco, but we'll all be dead."

Casey pulled up that Reno Hill,
He tooted for the crossing with an awful shrill,
The switchman knew by the engine's moan
That the man at the throttle was Casey Jones.
He pulled up within two miles of the place
Number Four stared him right in the face,
He turned to the fireman, said, "Boy, you better jump,
'Cause there's two locomotives that's a-goin' to bump":

Casey Jones, two locomotives,
Casey Jones, that's a-goin' to bump,
Casey Jones, two locomotives,
"There's two locomotives that's a-goin' to bump."

Casey said just before he died,
"There's two more roads that I'd like to ride."
The fireman said what could they be?
"The Southern Pacific and the Santa Fe."
Mrs Casey sat on her bed a-sighin',
Just received a message that Casey was dyin'.
Said, "Go to bed, children, and hush your cryin',
'Cause you got another papa on the Salt Lake Line":

Mrs Casey Jones, got another papa,
Mrs Casey Jones, on that Salt Lake Line,
Mrs Casey Jones, got another papa,
"And you've got another papa on the Salt Lake Line."

Anon

Take This Hammer

Take this hammer – huh!
And carry it to the captain – huh!
You tell him I'm gone – huh!
Tell him I'm gone – huh!

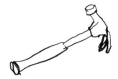

If he asks you – huh!
Was I runnin' – huh!
You tell him I was flyin' – huh!
Tell him I was flyin' – huh!

If he asks you – huh!
Was I laughin' – huh!
You tell him I was cryin' – huh!
You tell him I was cryin' – huh!

Anon

The Song of the Banana Man

Touris, white man, wipin his face,
Met me in Golden Grove market place.
He looked at m'ol' clothes brown wid stain,
An soaked right through wid de Portlan rain,
He cas his eye, turn up his nose,
He says, "You're a beggar man, I suppose?"
He says, "Boy, get some occupation,
Be of some value to your nation."
   I said, "By God and dis big right han
   You mus recognise a banana man.

"Up in de hills, where de streams are cool,
An mullet an janga swim in de pool,
I have ten acres of mountain side,
An a dainty-foot donkey dat I ride,
Four Gros Michel, an four Lacatan,
Some coconut trees, and some hills of yam,
An I pasture on dat very same lan
Five she-goats an a big black ram,
    Dat, by God an dis big right han
    Is de property of a banana man.

"I leave m'yard early-mornin time
An set m'foot to de mountain climb,
I ben m'back to de hot-sun toil,
An m'cutlass rings on de stony soil,
Ploughin an weedin, diggin an plantin
Till Massa Sun drop back o John Crow mountain,
Den home again in cool evenin time,
Perhaps whistling dis likkle rhyme,
    (Sung) Praise God an m'big right han
    I will live an die a banana man.

"Banana day is my special day,
I cut my stems an I'm on m'way,
Load up de donkey, leave de lan
Head down de hill to banana stan,
When de truck comes roun I take a ride
All de way down to de harbour side –
Dat is de night, when you, touris man,
Would change your place wid a banana man.
    Yes, by God, an m'big right han
    I will live an die a banana man.

"De bay is calm, an de moon is bright
De hills look black for de sky is light,
Down at de dock is an English ship,
Restin after her ocean trip,
While on de pier is a monstrous hustle,
Tallymen, carriers, all in a bustle,
Wid stems on deir heads in a long black snake
Some singin de songs dat banana men make,
   Like, (*Sung*) Praise God an m'big right han
   I will live an die a banana man.

"Den de payment comes, an we have some fun,
Me, Zekiel, Breda and Duppy Son.
Down at de bar near United Wharf
We knock back a white rum, bus a laugh,
Fill de empty bag for further toil
Wid saltfish, breadfruit, coconut oil.
Den head back home to m'yard to sleep,
A proper sleep dat is long an deep.
   Yes, by God, an m'big right han
   I will live an die a banana man.

"So when you see dese ol clothes brown wid stain,
An soaked right through wid de Portlan rain,
Don't cas your eye nor turn your nose,
Don't judge a man by his patchy clothes,
I'm a strong man, a proud man, an I'm free,
Free as dese mountains, free as dis sea,
I know myself, an I know my ways,
An will sing wid pride to de end o my days
   (*Sung*) Praise God an m'big right han
   I will live an die a banana man."

Evan Jones

All Over the World

women are knitting
in Ireland they are knitting thick
creamy cables each with their special stitch
so when their man is dragged out of the sea
with his face bloated purple
they will know him

in New York they are knitting on subways
with bright orange yarn stitch after
stitch and folding up their needles
tucking them into the plastic bag inside
a flowered plastic tote
in time to the train wheels as
the subway stops and they get off

in England they are knitting in airports
not only the English the Indians
the Pakistani the Americans they are
all sitting in Heathrow Airport knitting
long indecipherable scarves for persons
unknown

in Italy they are knitting black sweaters
for the saints with the methodical care
they perform upon their rosaries

women in Wales are knitting the dawn into
peat bog afghans girls in Ghana are
knitting tribal chieftans into unimagined
legends women in Chile are knitting
blood into the stockpile of tourniquets
waiting for the next round young women

in Istanbul are knitting far into the future
which is a replica of the past and it keeps
shrinking the closer they move into tomorrow

women in Iran are knitting insignias of the
oil companies to be sewn into the
covers for the coffins women in Ethiopia
are knitting green and white and red ribbons
to be worn around the hearts of those who
will not recognise the outcome

women in Russia are knitting peaceful parables
that will win the Nobel Prize
with long slavonic colours of melancholy
and hearty despair

women in Kansas are knitting according to the
latest catalogue in yellow and white
they are knitting strands of wheat into their
needles and they will
fill their kitchens with the abundance
that smiles because Kansas has not been bloody
since the time of the fierce old man John Brown

women in Amsterdam are knitting blue and white
porcelain doilies that are brittle and break
quickly unless purchased by tourists
their daughters are knitting with the
precision of an etching deep brown
quilts to cover themselves and their
lovers against the piercing sky

women in Paris are knitting bright Picasso
sweaters that they will never wear because
even now they do not know what makes them
choose those colours

women in the swamps and rivers of Indochina
are knitting the reeds and nettles into the
steel of machine gun bullets that will
explode with warmth into the bodies of
the men that are cold with the ignorance
of trespassing and long for comfort

girls in vacant towns
inbetween cities inbetween rivers on
maps are knitting their hopes in
small stitches echoing into each other
like muffled mirrors the needles
click smoothly in the language all
of the same word over and over
that no one can read the
same word over and over

Christina Starobin

Miners

There was a whispering in my hearth,
    A sigh of the coal,
Grown wistful of a former earth
    It might recall.

I listened for a tale of leaves
    And smothered ferns:
Frond-forests; and the low, sly lives
    Before the fawns.

My fire might show steam-phantoms simmer
　　From Time's old cauldron,
Before the birds made nests in summer,
　　Or men had children.

But the coals were murmuring of their mine,
　　And moans down there
Of boys that slept wry sleep, and men
　　Writhing for air.

And I saw white bones in the cinder-shard.
　　Bones without number;
For many hearts with coal are charred
　　And few remember.

I thought of some who worked dark pits
　　Or war, and died
Digging the rock where Death reputes
　　Peace lies indeed.

Comforted years will sit soft-chaired
　　In rooms of amber;
The years will stretch their hands, well-cheered
　　By our lives' ember.

The centuries will burn rich loads
　　With which we groaned,
Whose warmth shall lull their dreaming lids
　　While songs are crooned.
But they will not dream of us poor lads
　　Lost in the ground.

Wilfred Owen

The Lincolnshire Poacher

When I was bound apprentice, in famous Lincolnshire,
Full well I served my master for more than seven year,
Till I took up to poaching, as you shall quickly hear:
Oh, 'tis my delight on a shining night, in the season of the year.

As me and my companions were setting of a snare,
'Twas then we spied the gamekeeper, for him we did not care.
For we can wrestle and fight, my boys, and jump out anywhere;
Oh, 'tis my delight on a shining night, in the season of the year.

As me and my companions were setting four or five,
And, taking on 'em up again, we caught a hare alive.
We took the hare alive, my boys, and through the wood did steer:
Oh, 'tis my delight on a shining night, in the season of the year.

I threw him on my shoulder, and then we trudgèd home,
We took him to a neighbour's house and sold him for a crown,
We sold him for a crown, my boys, but I did not tell you where:
Oh, 'tis my delight on a shining night, in the season of the year.

Success to every gentleman that lives in Lincolnshire,
Success to every poacher that wants to sell a hare,
Bad luck to every gamekeeper that will not sell his deer:
Oh, 'tis my delight on a shining night, in the season of the year.

Anon

The Justice of the Peace

Distinguish carefully between these two,
    This thing is yours, that other thing is mine.
You have a shirt, a brimless hat, a shoe
    And half a coat. I am the Lord benign
Of fifty hundred acres of fat land
To which I have a right. You understand?

I have a right because I have, because,
    Because I have – because I have a right.
Now be quite calm and good, obey the laws,
    Remember your low station, do not fight
Against the goad, because, you know, it pricks
Whenever the uncleanly demos kicks.

I do not envy you your hat, your shoe.
    Why should you envy me my small estate?
It's fearfully illogical in you
    To fight with economic force and fate.
Moreover, I have got the upper hand,
And mean to keep it. Do you understand?

Hilaire Belloc

Heaven-Haven
A Nun Takes the Veil

I have desired to go
    Where springs not fail,
To fields where flies no sharp and sided hail
    And a few lilies blow.

And I have asked to be
    Where no storms come,
Where the green swell is in the havens dumb,
    And out of the swing of the sea.

Gerard Manley Hopkins

Old Shepherd's Prayer

Up to the bed by the window, where I be lyin',
Comes bells and bleat of the flock wi' they two children's clack.
Over, from under the eaves there's the starlings flyin',
And down in yard, fit to burst his chain, yapping out at Sue I do hear
    young Mac.

Turning around like a falled-over sack
I can see team ploughin' in Whithy-bush field and meal carts startin' up
    road to Church-Town;
Saturday arternoon the men goin' back
And the women from market, trapin' home over the down.

Heavenly Master, I wud like to wake to they same green places
Where I be know'd for breakin' dogs and follerin' sheep.
And if I may not walk in th' old ways and look on th' old faces
I wud sooner sleep.

Charlotte Mew

King of the Road

Trailer for sale or rent,
Rooms to let fifty cents,
No phone, no pool, no pets,
I ain't got no cigarettes.
Ah, but two hours of pushing broom buys a
Eight-by-twelve four-bit room
I'm a man of means by no means
King of the Road.

Third box car midnight train
Destination Bangor, Maine,
Old worn-out suit and shoes,
I don't pay no union dues.
I smoke old stogies I have found,
Short but not too big around.
I'm a man of means by no means
King of the Road.

I know every engineer on every train
All of the children and all of their names
And every handout in every town
And every lock that ain't locked when no one's around.

I sing, "Trailer for sale or rent,
Rooms to let fifty cents,"
No phone, no pool, no pets,
I ain't got no cigarettes.
Ah, but two hours of pushing broom buys a
Eight-by-twelve four-bit room
I'm a man of means by no means
King of the Road.

Roger Miller

Things Men Have Made —

Things men have made with wakened hands, and put soft life into
are awake through years with transferred touch, and go on glowing
for long years.
And for this reason, some old things are lovely
warm still with the life of forgotten men who made them.

Things Made by Iron —

Things made by iron and handled by steel
are born dead, they are shrouds, they soak life out of us.
Till after a long time, when they are old and have steeped in our life
they begin to be soothed and soothing: then we throw them away.

New Houses, New Clothes —

New houses, new furniture, new streets, new clothes, new sheets
everything new and machine-made sucks life out of us
and makes us cold, makes us lifeless
the more we have.

Whatever Man Makes —

Whatever man makes and makes it live
lives because of the life put into it.
A yard of India muslin is alive with Hindu life.
And a Navajo woman, weaving her rug in the pattern of her dream
must run the pattern out in a little break at the end
so that her soul can come out, back to her.

But in the odd pattern, like snake-marks on the sand
it leaves its trail.

D. H. Lawrence

Spectator Ab Extra

As I sat at the café I said to myself,
They may talk as they please about what they call pelf,
They may sneer as they like about eating and drinking,
But help it I cannot, I cannot help thinking,
　　How pleasant it is to have money, heigh-ho!
　　How pleasant it is to have money.

I sit at my table *en grand seigneur*,
And when I have done, throw a crust to the poor;
Not only the pleasure, one's self, of good living,
But also the pleasure of now and then giving.
　　So pleasant it is to have money, heigh-ho!
　　So pleasant it is to have money.

They may talk as they please about what they call pelf,
And how one ought never to think of one's self,
How pleasures of thought surpass eating and drinking –
My pleasure of thought is the pleasure of thinking
　　How pleasant it is to have money, heigh-ho!
　　How pleasant it is to have money.

Arthur Hugh Clough

Job Hunting

On the wasteland that stretches
From here to the river
My children play a game.
It is called job hunting.
They blacken their faces,
And with knives and imitation guns
They go stalking among
The lichen-coated ruins
Of broken machinery and cranes.
It is an exciting game.
Sometimes they come back exhausted,
Clutching objects they have prised
From the earth –
Nuts, bolts, the broken vizor
Of a welder's mask.
"Daddy," they ask, "Daddy,
Is this a job? Can we keep it?"

Brian Patten

The Crazy River

Riddles and Utter Nonsense

The Frog

What a wonderful bird the frog are.
When he sit he stand almost.
When he hop he fly almost.
He ain't got no sense hardly.
He ain't got no tail hardly neither
Where he sit almost.

Anon

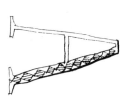

What's in There?

What's in there?
Gold and money.
Where's my share of it?
The moosie ran awa' wi't.
Where's the moosie?
In her hoosie.
Where's her hoosie?
In the wood.
Where's the wood?
The fire burnt it.
Where's the fire?
The water quenched it.
Where's the water?
The broon bull drank it.
Where's the broon bull?
Back o' Burnie's hill.
Where's Burnie's hill?
A'clad wi' snaw.
Where's the snaw?
The sun melted it.
Where's the sun?
High, high, up i' the air!

Anon

What Is Pink?

What is pink? a rose is pink
By the fountain's brink.
What is red? a poppy's red
In its barley bed.
What is blue? the sky is blue
Where the clouds float thro'
What is white? a swan is white
Sailing in the light.
What is yellow? pears are yellow,
Rich and ripe and mellow.
What is green? the grass is green,
With small flowers between.
What is violet? clouds are violet
In the summer twilight.
What is orange? why, an orange,
Just an orange!

Christina Rossetti

Snow and Sun

White bird, featherless,
Flew from Paradise,
Pitched on the castle wall;
Along came Lord Landless,
Took it up handless,
And rode away horseless to the King's white hall.

Anon

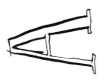

Sensitive, Seldom and Sad

Sensitive, Seldom and Sad are we,
As we wend our way to the sneezing sea,
With our hampers full of thistles and fronds
To plant round the edge of the dab-fish ponds;
Oh, so Sensitive, Seldom and Sad –
Oh, *so* Seldom and Sad.

In the shambling shades of the shelving shore,
We will sing us a song of the Long Before,
And light a red fire and warm our paws
For it's chilly, it is, on the Desolate shores,
For those who are Sensitive, Seldom and Sad,
For those who are Seldom and Sad.

Sensitive, Seldom and Sad we are,
As we wander along through Lands Afar,
To the sneezing sea, where the sea-weeds be,
And the dab-fish ponds that are waiting for we
Who are, Oh, so Sensitive, Seldom and Sad,
Oh, *so* Seldom and Sad.

Mervyn Peake

I Cannot Give the Reasons

I cannot give the reasons,
I only sing the tunes:
the sadness of the seasons
the madness of the moons.

I cannot be didactic
or lucid, but I can
be quite obscure and practically marzipan

In gorgery and gushness
and all that's squishified.
My voice has all the lushness
of what I can't abide

And yet it has a beauty
most proud and terrible
denied to those whose duty
is to be cerebral.

Among the antlered mountains
I make my viscous way
and watch the sepia fountains
throw up their lime-green spray.

Mervyn Peake

A is for Parrot

A is for Parrot which we can plainly see

B is for glasses which we can plainly see

C is for plastic which we can plainly see

D is for Doris

E is for binoculars I'll get it in five

F is for Ethel who lives next door

G is for orange which we love to eat when we can get
them because they come from abroad

H is for England and (Heather)

I is for monkey we see in the tree

J is for parrot which we can plainly see

K is for shoetop we wear to the ball

L is for Land because brown

M is for Venezuela where the oranges come from

N is for Brazil near Venezuela (very near)

O is for football which we kick about a bit

T is for Tommy who won the war

Q is a garden which we can plainly see

R is for intestines which hurt when we dance

S is for pancake or whole-wheat bread

U is for Ethel who lives on the hill

P is arab and her sister will

V is for me

W is for lighter which never lights

X is for easter – have one yourself

Y is a crooked letter and you can't straighten it

Z is for Apple which we can plainly see

This is my story both humble and true

Take it to pieces and mend it with glue

John Lennon

The White Knight's Song

I'll tell thee everything I can;
　　There's little to relate.
I saw an aged aged man,
　　A-sitting on a gate.
"Who are you, aged man?" I said,
　　"And how is it you live?"
And his answer trickled through my head
　　Like water through a sieve.

He said "I look for butterflies
　　That sleep among the wheat:
I make them into mutton-pies,
　　And sell them in the street.
I sell them unto men," he said,
　　"Who sail on stormy seas;
And that's the way I get my bread –
　　A trifle, if you please."

But I was thinking of a plan
　　To dye one's whiskers green,
And always use so large a fan
　　That they could not be seen.
So, having no reply to give
　　To what the old man said,
I cried "Come, tell me how you live!"
　　And thumped him on the head.

His accents mild took up the tale:
   He said "I go my ways,
And when I find a mountain-rill,
   I set it in a blaze;
And thence they make a stuff they call
   Rowland's Macassar-Oil –
Yet twopence-halfpenny is all
   They give me for my toil."

But I was thinking of a way
   To feed oneself on batter,
And so go on from day to day
   Getting a little fatter.
I shook him well from side to side,
   Until his face was blue:
"Come, tell me how you live," I cried,
   "And, what it is you do!"

He said "I hunt for haddocks' eyes
   Among the heather bright,
And work them into waistcoat-buttons
   In the silent night.
And these I do not sell for gold
   Or coin of silvery shine,
But for a copper halfpenny,
   And that will purchase nine.

"I sometimes dig for buttered rolls,
   Or set limed twigs for crabs;
I sometimes search the grassy knolls
   For wheels of Hansom-cabs.
And that's the way" (he gave a wink)
   "By which I get my wealth –
And very gladly will I drink
   Your Honour's noble health."

I heard him then, for I had just
   Completed my design
To keep the Menai bridge from rust
   By boiling it in wine.
I thanked him much for telling me
   The way he got his wealth,
But chiefly for his wish that he
   Might drink my noble health.

And now, if e'er by chance I put
   My fingers into glue,
Or madly squeeze a right-hand foot
   Into a left-hand shoe,
Or if I drop upon my toe
   A very heavy weight,
I weep, for it reminds me so
Of that old man I used to know –
Whose look was mild, whose speech was slow,
Whose hair was whiter than the snow,
Whose face was very like a crow,
With eyes, like cinders, all aglow,
Who seemed distracted with his woe,
Who rocked his body to and fro,
And muttered mumblingly and low,
As if his mouth were full of dough,
Who snorted like a buffalo –
That summer evening long ago
   A-sitting on a gate.

Lewis Carroll

He Thought He Saw an Elephant

He thought he saw an Elephant,
   That practised on a fife:
He looked again, and found it was
   A letter from his wife.
"At length I realise," he said,
   "The bitterness of Life!"

He thought he saw a Buffalo
   Upon the chimney-piece:
He looked again, and found it was
   His Sister's Husband's Niece.
"Unless you leave this house," he said,
   "I'll send for the Police!"

He thought he saw a Rattlesnake
   That questioned him in Greek:
He looked again, and found it was
   The Middle of Next Week.
"The one thing I regret," he said,
   "Is that it cannot speak!"

He thought he saw a Banker's Clerk
   Descending from the bus:
He looked again, and found it was
   A Hippopotamus:
"If this should stay to dine," he said,
   "There won't be much for us!"

He thought he saw a Kangaroo
   That worked a coffee-mill:

He looked again, and found it was
    A Vegetable-Pill.
"Were I to swallow this," he said,
    "I should be very ill!"

He thought he saw a Coach-and-Four
    That stood beside his bed:
He looked again and found it was
    A Bear without a Head.
"Poor thing," he said, "Poor silly thing!
    "It's waiting to be fed!"

He thought he saw an Albatross
    That fluttered round the lamp:
He looked again, and found it was
    A Penny-Postage-Stamp.
"You'd best be getting home," he said:
    "The nights are very damp!"

He thought he saw a Garden-Door
    That opened with a key:
He looked again, and found it was
    A Double Rule of Three:
"And all its mystery," he said,
    "Is clear as day to me!"

He thought he saw an Argument
    That proved he was the Pope:
He looked again, and found it was
    A Bar of Mottled Soap.
"A fact so dread," he faintly said,
    "Extinguishes all hope!"

Lewis Carroll

Scorflufus
By a well-known National Health Victim
No. 3908631

There are many diseases,
That strike people's kneeses,
Scorflufus! is one by name
It comes from the East
Packed in bladders of yeast
So the Chinese must take half the blame.

There's a case in the files
Of Sir Barrington-Pyles
While hunting a fox one day
Shot up in the air
And *remained hanging there!*
While the hairs on his socks turned grey!

Aye! Scorflufus had struck!
At man, beast and duck.
And the knees of the world went Bong!
Some knees went Ping!
Other knees turned to string
From Balham to old Hong-Kong.

Should you hold your life dear,
Then the remedy's clear,
If you're offered some yeast – don't eat it!
Turn the offer down flat –
Don your travelling hat –
Put an egg in your boot – and beat it!

Spike Milligan

Look Ahead

Our toes are ahead of us – they have grown out of us

Our nails are ahead of our toes – we can't reach to cut them

Our hammers are ahead of our nails – they strike
   like underpaid lightning

Our sickles are ahead of our hammers – shape of our hammer toes

Our televisions are ahead of our cinemas – our films are because
   we don't use good toothpaste
   state and church fight tooth and nail
   whilst producers forge ahead of viewers

Our commercials are ahead of our patrons –
   all is peddled

Our cycles are ahead of our tricycles and our trickles are
   our fashionable works of art
   trickled by cyclists on paint

Our best cyclists are our worst painters and

Our best painters are worse than our worst cyclists –

Our worst cyclists are ahead of all our painters
   put together – save the painters become cyclists
   and that's what they've done –
   every day more painters are taking up cycling
   and daily they are discovered
   biking up the strand –

sponsored they swerve through swirls of paint
dribble ahead of trolleys trams trombones –
start brushing their feet with toothpaste
that the Tour de France is gunged to a standstill
whilst cinemas clean up with the masses at bingo
and the backsliding punter lies down with the telly –

Our piledriver toes hammer furiously on motorcycles
but the hammers are sliced by sickles
struck hard by

Our frames our nails catch up with our toes till at last
we're in –
we find our – teeth
fully grown

footballers

Michael Horovitz

Self-Portrait of the Laureate of Nonsense

How pleasant to know Mr Lear!
    Who has written such volumes of stuff!
Some think him ill-tempered and queer,
    But a few think him pleasant enough.

His mind is concrete and fastidious,
    His nose is remarkably big;
His visage is more or less hideous,
    His beard it resembles a wig.

He has ears, and two eyes, and ten fingers,
    Leastways if you reckon two thumbs;
Long ago he was one of the singers,
    But now he is one of the dumbs.

He sits in a beautiful parlour,
    With hundreds of books on the wall;
He drinks a great deal of Marsala,
    But never gets tipsy at all.

He has many friends, laymen and clerical;
    Old Foss is the name of his cat;
His body is perfectly spherical,
    He weareth a runcible hat.

When he walks in a waterproof white,
    The children run after him so!
Calling out, "He's come out in his night-
    Gown, that crazy old Englishman, oh!"

He weeps by the side of the ocean,
    He weeps on the top of the hill;
He purchases pancakes and lotion,
    And chocolate shrimps from the mill.

He reads but he cannot speak Spanish,
    He cannot abide ginger-beer:
Ere the days of his pilgrimage vanish,
    How pleasant to know Mr Lear!

Edward Lear

The Pobble Who Has No Toes

The Pobble who has no toes
    Had once as many as we;
When they said, "Some day you may lose them all" –
    He replied, "Fish fiddle de-dee!"
And his Aunt Jobiska made him drink,
Lavender water tinged with pink,
For she said, "The World in general knows
There's nothing so good for a Pobble's toes!"

The Pobble who has no toes,
    Swam across the Bristol Channel;
But before he set out he wrapped his nose,
    In a piece of scarlet flannel.
For his Aunt Jobiska said, "No harm
Can come to his toes if his nose is warm;
And it's perfectly known that a Pobble's toes
Are safe – provided he minds his nose."

The Pobble swam fast and well
    And when boats or ships came near him
He tinkledy-binkledy-winkled a bell
    So that all the world could hear him.
And all the Sailors and Admirals cried,
When they saw him nearing the further side –
"He has gone to fish, for his Aunt Jobiska's
Runcible Cat with crimson whiskers!"

But before he touched the shore,
    The shore of the Bristol Channel,
A sea-green Porpoise carried away
    His wrapper of scarlet flannel.
And when he came to observe his feet

Formerly garnished with toes so neat
His face at once became forlorn
On perceiving that all his toes were gone!

And nobody ever knew
   From that dark day to the present,
Whoso had taken the Pobble's toes,
   In a manner so far from pleasant.
Whether the shrimps or crawfish gray,
Or crafty Mermaids stole them away –
Nobody knew; and nobody knows
How the Pobble was robbed of his twice five toes!

The Pobble who has no toes
   Was placed in a friendly Bark,
And they rowed him back, and carried him up,
   To his Aunt Jobiska's Park.
And she made him a feast at his earnest wish
Of eggs and buttercups fried with fish –
And she said, "It's a fact the whole world knows,
That Pobbles are happier without their toes."

Edward Lear

Hallelujah!

   "Hallelujah!" was the only observation
That escaped Lieutenant-Colonel Mary Jane,
When she tumbled off the platform in the station,
And was cut in little pieces by the train.
   Mary Jane, the train is through yer:
   Hallelujah, Hallelujah!
We will gather up the fragments that remain.

A. E. Housman

Alternative Endings to an Unwritten Ballad

I stole through the dungeons, while everyone slept,
    Till I came to the cage where the Monster was kept.
There, locked in the arms of a Giant Baboon,
    Rigid and smiling, lay . . . MRS RAVOON!

I climbed the clock tower in the first morning sun
    And 'twas midday at least 'ere my journey was done;
But the clock never sounded the last stroke of noon,
    For there, from the clapper, swung MRS RAVOON!

I hauled in the line, and I took my first look
    At the half-eaten horror that hung from the hook.
I had dragged from the depths of the limpid lagoon
    The luminous body of MRS RAVOON.

I fled in the storm, the lightning and thunder,
    And there, as a flash split the darkness asunder,
Chewing a rat's-tail and mumbling a rune,
    Mad in the moat squatted MRS RAVOON!

I stood by the waters so green and so thick,
    And I stirred at the scum with my old, withered stick;
When there rose through the ooze, like a monstrous balloon,
    The bloated cadaver of MRS RAVOON.

Facing the fens, I looked back from the shore
    Where all had been empty a moment before;
And there by the light of the Lincolnshire moon,
    Immense on the marshes, stood . . . MRS RAVOON!

Paul Dehn

The Road to Jeopardy

Dangerous Journeys
Desperate Criminals
and Life on the High Seas

Thoughts of a Module

It is black so. There is that dust.
My ladder in light. What are my men.
One is foot down. That is pack drill.
Black what is vizor. A hiss I heard.
The talks go up. Clump now but float.
Is a jump near. A camera paced out.
I phase another man. Another man is second.
Second last feet on. The dust I think.
So some soles cross. Is a flag near.
No move yon flag. Which voice comes down.
White house thanks all. Command module man not.
Is kangaroo hop around. I think moon dance.
Or white bird is. Good oxygen I heard.
Earth monitors must be. Is it too pressing.
Trained man is gay. Fail safe is gay.
The black I see. What instruments are lonely.
Sharp is a shadow. A horizon goes flat.
All rock are samples. Dust taken I think.
Is bright my leg. In what sun yonder.
An end I think. How my men go.
The talks come down. The ladder I shake.
To leave that bright. Space dark I see.
Is my men last. Men are that first.
That moon is there. They have some dust.
Is home they know. Blue earth I think.
I lift I see. It is that command.
My men go back. I leave that there.
It is bright so.

Edwin Morgan

192

Stars and Planets

Trees are cages for them: water holds its breath
To balance them without smudging on its delicate meniscus.
Children watch them playing in their heavenly playground;
Men use them to lug ships across oceans, through firths.

They seem so twinkle-still, but they never cease
Inventing new spaces and huge explosions
And migrating in mathematical tribes over
The steppes of space at their outrageous ease.

It's hard to think that the earth is one –
This poor sad bearer of wars and disasters
Rolls-Roycing round the sun with its load of gangsters,
Attended only by the loveless moon.

Norman MacCaig

Uphill

Does the road wind uphill all the way?
   Yes, to the very end.
Will the day's journey take the whole long day?
   From morn to night, my friend.

But is there for the night a resting-place?
   A roof for when the slow, dark hours begin.
May not the darkness hide it from my face?
   You cannot miss that inn.

Shall I meet other wayfarers at night?
   Those who have gone before.
Then must I knock, or call when just in sight?
   They will not keep you waiting at that door.

Shall I find comfort, travel-sore and weak?
   Of labour you shall find the sum.
Will there be beds for me and all who seek?
   Yea, beds for all who come.

Christina Rossetti

Message from the Border

A messenger,
>
> bald, his skin burnt onto his bones, he appears on the skyrim
> walking, not slowly nor fast, just walking: his bones move,
> his toe-joints grip the ground: he has been on his way,
> he will soon arrive,

We see him approach,
>
> we will see him arrive, we are his arrival: we will see
> how he opens his mouth, we will say: no! first – drink this!
> we will see how the water runs down into this sun-crumpled hide,
> filling out a few wrinkles,

And he will open his mouth
>
> and deliver the message: what will he say?

He will say what the one before him said,
>
> and the one before that one – he will tell us! The dancers! –
> the dancers – they – are surrounded! by the burning –

So simple it hurts . . . and always the same.
What else could it be?
What else could the messenger say
>
> these days? The dancers, in the midst of the burning . . .
>> this
> is the messenger's voice, the sound of his horn, abandoned
> for lightness, and speed, now it lies on the sand
> cracked by the heat, blackened – soon charred
> by the black
> heat

Anselm Hollo

The Jungle Husband

Dearest Evelyn, I often think of you

Out with the guns in the jungle stew

Yesterday I hittapotamus

I put the measurements down for you but they got lost in
the fuss

It's not a good thing to drink out here

You know, I've practically given it up dear.

Tomorrow I am going alone a long way

Into the jungle. It is all grey

But green on top

Only sometimes when a tree has fallen

The sun comes down plop, it is quite appalling.

You never want to go in a jungle pool

In the hot sun, it would be the act of a fool

Because it's always full of anacondas, Evelyn, not looking
ill-fed

I'll say. So no more now, from your loving husband,
Wilfred.

Stevie Smith

Ozymandias

I met a traveller from an antique land
Who said: Two vast and trunkless legs of stone
Stand in the desert . . . Near them, on the sand,
Half sunk, a shattered visage lies, whose frown,
And wrinkled lip, and sneer of cold command,
Tell that its sculptor well those passions read
Which yet survive, stamped on these lifeless things,
The hand that mocked them, and the heart that fed:
And on the pedestal these words appear:
"My name is Ozymandias, king of kings:
Look on my works, ye Mighty, and despair!"
Nothing beside remains. Round the decay
Of that colossal wreck, boundless and bare
The lone and level sands stretch far away.

Percy Bysshe Shelley

The Terrible Path

While playing at the woodland's edge
I saw a child one day,
She was standing near a foaming brook
And a sign half-rotted away.

There was something strange about her clothes;
They were from another age,
I might have seen them in a book
Upon a mildewed page.

She looked pale and frightened,
Her voice was thick with dread.
She spoke through lips rimmed with green
And this is what she said:

"I saw a signpost with no name,
I was surprised and had to stare,
It pointed to a broken gate
And a path that led nowhere.

"The path had run to seed and I
Walked as in a dream.
It entered a silent oak wood,
And crossed a silent stream.

"And in a tree a silent bird
Mouthed a silent song.
I wanted to turn back again
But something had gone wrong.

"The path would not let me go;
It had claimed me for its own,
It led me through a dark wood
Where all was overgrown.

"I followed it until the leaves
Had fallen from the trees,
I followed it until the frost
Drugged the autumn's bees.

"I followed it until the spring
Dissolved the winter snow,
And whichever way it turned
I was obliged to go.

"The years passed like shooting stars,
They melted and were gone,
But the path itself seemed endless,
It twisted and went on.

"I followed it and thought aloud,
'I'll be found, wait and see.'
Yet in my heart I knew by then
The world had forgotten me."

Frightened I turned homeward,
But stopped and had to stare.
I too saw that signpost with no name,
And the path that led nowhere.

Brian Patten

Frankie and Johnny

Frankie and Johnny were lovers,
Oh Lord how they could love,
Swore to be true to each other,
True as the stars above.
  He was her man,
  But he done her wrong.

Frankie was a good woman,
As everybody knows,
She'd give her man a hundred dollars
Just to buy a suit of clothes.
  He was her man,
  But he done her wrong.

Frankie she went to Memphis –
She went on the morning train –
She paid a hundred dollars
For Johnny a watch and chain.
  He was her man,
  But he done her wrong.

Frankie went down to the corner
Just to fetch her a bucket of beer,
She said to the barman: "Freddie –
Has my lover Johnny been here?
　　He is my man,
　　He wouldn't do me wrong."

"I don't wanna tell you no story.
Don't wanna tell you no lie.
But I saw Johnny 'bout an hour ago
With that damn Nelly Bly.
　　He is your man,
　　But he's doing you wrong."

Frankie went down to the pawn-shop,
Bought her a little forty-four.
She aimed it at the ceiling
And shot a big hole in the floor.
　　"Where is my man?
　　B'lieve he's doing me wrong."

Frankie went down to the bar-room,
Didn't stop to ring the bell.
She said: "Stand back all you pimps and whores
Or I'll blow you all to hell!
　　I want my man,
　　He's been doing me wrong."

Frankie looked over the transom,
Oh, what a sight met her eye.
Down on a couch sat Johnny,
Making up to Nelly Bly.
   He was her man,
   He was doing her wrong.

Frankie pulled back her kimono,
Took out her little forty-four.
Rooty-toot-toot three times she shot
Right through that hardwood door.
   She shot her man
   'Cause he done her wrong.

"Roll me over easy,
Roll me over slow.
Roll me over on my left side
For your bullets are hurting me so.
   I was your man
   Though I done you wrong."

Johnny he was a gambler,
He gambled for the gain.
The very last words he ever said were:
"High-low Jack and the game."
   He was her man,
   But he done her wrong.

The first shot, Johnny staggered.
The second shot, he fell.
The third shot, Frankie fired at him.
Then was a new man's face in Hell.
    He was her man,
    But he done her wrong.

Frankie she went to the river,
She looked from bank to bank.
"Do all you can for a gambling man
But you will get no thanks.
    He was my man,
    But he done me wrong."

Frankie she looked down Main Street,
Far as the eye could see.
All she could hear was a one-string guitar
Playing 'Nearer O My God to Thee'.
    He was her man,
    But he done her wrong.

"Bring round your rubber-tyred hearses.
Bring round your rubber-tyred hack.
I'm taking my man to the boneyard
And I ain't gonna bring him back.
    He was my man,
    Though he done me wrong."

"Bring round a thousand policemen,
Bring 'em round today.
Oh, lock me up in a dungeon cell
And throw the key away.
   I shot my man,
   But he done me wrong.

"Yes, put me down in that dungeon,
Lock me up in that cell.
Put me where the north wind blows
From the south-east corner of Hell.
   I shot my man
   When he done me wrong."

The Judge he said to Frankie:
"Explain it if you can."
Frankie looked him straight in the eye,
Said: "I shot my lovin' man.
   He was my man,
   But he done me wrong."

Now it wasn't murder in the second degree,
Was not murder in the third.
Frankie simply shot her man
Like a hunter drops a bird.
   He was her man,
   But he done her wrong.

Now the last time I saw Frankie
She was sitting in the 'lectric chair.
She was crying out for Johnny
And the sparks were in her hair.
　She shot her man,
　But he done her wrong.

This story has no moral,
This story has no end.
This story only goes to show
That there ain't no good in men.
　He was her man,
　But he done her wrong.

Anon

My Bonny Black Bess

Let the lover his mistress's beauty rehearse,
And laud her attractions in languishing verse;
Be it mine in rude strain but with truth to express
The love that I bear to my Bonny Black Bess.

From the West was her dam, from the East was her sire;
From the one came her swiftness, the other her fire;
No peer of the realm better blood can possess
Than flows in the blood of my Bonny Black Bess.

Look! Look! how that eyeball glows bright as a brand,
That neck proudly arching, those nostrils expand;
Mark that wide flowing mane, of which each silky tress
Might adorn prouder beauties, though none like Black Bess.

Mark that skin sleek as velvet and dusky as night,
With its jet undisfigured by one lock of white,
That throat branched with veins, prompt to charge or caress,
Now is she not beautiful, Bonny Black Bess?

Over·highway and byway, in rough or smooth weather,
Some thousands of miles have we journeyed together;
Our couch the same straw, our meals the same mess,
No couple more constant than I and Black Bess.

By moonlight, in darkness, by night and by day
Her headlong career there is nothing can stay;
She cares not for distance, she knows not distress.
Can you show me a courser to match with Black Bess?

Once it happened in Cheshire, near Durham, I popped
On a horseman alone whom I suddenly stopped;
That I lightened his pockets you'll readily guess –
Quick work makes Dick Turpin when mounted on Bess.

Now it seems the man knew me: "Dick Turpin," said he,
"You shall swing for this job, as you live, d'ye see?"
I laughed at his threats and his vows of redress –
I was sure of an alibi then with Black Bess.

Brake, brook, meadow, and ploughed field Bess fleetly bestrode;
As the crow wings his flight we selected our road.
We arrived at Hough Green in five minutes or less,
My neck it was saved by the speed of Black Bess.

Stepping carelessly forward I lounge on the green,
Taking excellent care that by all I am seen;
Some remarks on time's flight to the squires I address;
But I say not a word of the flight of Black Bess.

I mention the hour – it is just about four,
Play a rubber at bowls, think the danger is o'er,
When athwart my next game like a checkmate in chess
Comes the horseman in search of the rider of Bess.

What matter details? Off with triumph I came.
He swears to the hour and the squires swear the same.
I had robbed him at four, while at four, they profess
I was quietly bowling – all thanks to Black Bess.

Then one halloo, boys, one loud cheering halloo,
For the swiftest of coursers, the gallant, the true,
For the sportsman inborn shall the memory bless
Of the horse of the highwaymen, Bonny Black Bess.

Anon

Lord Randal

"O where hae ye been, Lord Randal, my son?
  O where hae ye been, my handsome young man?"
"I hae been to the wild wood; mother, make my bed soon,
  For I'm weary wi' hunting, and fain wald lie down."

"Where gat ye your dinner, Lord Randal, my son?
  Where gat ye your dinner, my handsome young man?"
"I din'd wi' my true-love; mother, make my bed soon,
  For I'm weary wi' hunting, and fain wald lie down."

"What gat ye to your dinner, Lord Randal, my son?
  What gat ye to your dinner, my handsome young man?"
"I gat eels boil'd in broo; mother, make my bed soon,
  For I'm weary wi' hunting, and fain wald lie down."

"What became of your bloodhounds, Lord Randal, my son?
  What became of your bloodhounds, my handsome young man?"
"O they swell'd and they died; mother, make my bed soon,
  For I'm weary wi' hunting, and fain wald lie down."

"O I fear ye are poisoned, Lord Randal, my son!
  O I fear ye are poisoned, my handsome young man!"
"O yes! I am poison'd; mother, make my bed soon,
  For I'm sick at the heart, and fain wald lie down."

Anon

Henry My Son

"Where have you been all the day,
Henry my son?
Where have you been all the day,
My handsome one?"

"In the woods, dear Mother.
In the woods, dear Mother.
Oh, Mother, be quick
I'm going to be sick
And lay me down to die."

"Oh, what did you do in the woods,
Henry my boy?
What did you do in the woods,
My pride and joy?"

"Ate, dear Mother.
Ate, dear Mother.
Oh, Mother, be quick
I'm going to be sick
And lay me down to die."

"Oh, what did you eat in the woods,
Henry my son?
What did you eat in the woods,
My handsome one?"

"Eels, dear Mother.
Eels, dear Mother.
Oh, Mother, be quick
I'm going to be sick
And lay me down to die."

"Oh, what colour was them eels,
Henry my boy?
What colour was them eels,
My pride and joy?"

"Green and yeller!
Green and yeller!
Oh, Mother, be quick
I'm going to be sick
And lay me down to die."

"Them eels was snakes,
Henry my son.
Them eels was snakes,
My handsome one."

"Yerr-uck! dear Mother.
Yerr-uck! dear Mother.
Oh, Mother, be quick
I'm going to be sick
And lay me down to die."

"Oh, what colour flowers would you like,
Henry my son?
What colour flowers would you like,
My handsome one?"

"Green and yeller.
Green and yeller.
Oh, Mother, be quick
I'm going to be sick
And lay me down to die."

Anon

At the Railway Station, Upway

"There is not much that I can do,
    For I've no money that's quite my own!"
    Spoke up the pitying child –
A little boy with a violin
At the station before the train came in –
"But I can play my fiddle to you,
And a nice one 'tis, and good in tone!"

    The man in the handcuffs smiled;
The constable looked, and he smiled, too,
    As the fiddle began to twang;
And the man in the handcuffs suddenly sang
            With grimful glee:
            "This life so free
            Is the thing for me!"
And the constable smiled, and said no word,
As if unconscious of what he heard;
And so they went on till the train came in –
The convict, and boy with the violin.

Thomas Hardy

Frank Carew Macgraw

The name of Frank Carew Macgraw
Was notorious in the West,
Not as the fastest on the draw
But 'cause he only wore a vest.

Yes just a vest and nothing more!
Through the Wild and Woolly West,
They knew the name of Frank Macgraw
'Cause he only wore a vest.

Oh! His nether parts swung wild and free
As on his horse he sat.
He wore a vest and nothing else –
Oh! except a cowboy hat.

Yes! naked from the waist he rode –
He did not give two hoots!
Frank Macgraw in hat and vest
Oh! and a pair of boots.

But nothing else – no! not a stitch!
As through the cactus he
Rode on his horse, although of course
He did protect his knee

With leather leggings – but that's all!
No wonder that his name
Was infamous throughout the West
And spoken of with shame.

Actually he *did* wear pants
On Sunday, and it's true
He also wore them other days –
And sometimes he wore two!

And often in an overcoat
You'd see him riding by,
But as he went men shook their heads
And ladies winked their eye,

For *everyone* knew Frank Macgraw
Throughout the Old Wild West –
Not because he broke the law
But 'cause he *only* wore a vest!

Terry Jones

The Frivolous Cake

A freckled and frivolous cake there was
    That sailed on a pointless sea,
Or any lugubrious lake there was,
    In a manner emphatic and free.
How jointlessly, and how jointlessly
    The frivolous cake sailed by
On the waves of the ocean that pointlessly
    Threw fish to the lilac sky.

Oh, plenty and plenty of hake there was
    Of a glory beyond compare,
And every conceivable make there was
    Was tossed through the lilac air.

Up the smooth billows and over the crests
    Of the cumbersome combers flew
The frivolous cake with a knife in the wake
    Of herself and her curranty crew.

Like a swordfish grim it would bounce and skim
    (This dinner knife fierce and blue),
And the frivolous cake was filled to the brim
    With the fun of her curranty crew.

Oh, plenty and plenty of hake there was
    Of a glory beyond compare –
And every conceivable make there was
    Was tossed through the lilac air.

Around the shores of the Elegant Isles
    Where the cat-fish bask and purr
And lick their paws with adhesive smiles

And wriggle their fins of fur,
They fly and fly 'neath the lilac sky –
  The frivolous cake and the knife
Who winketh his glamorous indigo eye
  In the wake of his future wife.

The crumbs blow free down the pointless sea
  To the beat of a cakey heart
And the sensitive steel of the knife can feel
  That love is a race apart.
In the speed of the lingering light are blown
  The crumbs to the hake above,
And the tropical air vibrates to the drone
  Of a cake in the throes of love.

Mervyn Peake

Profoundly True Reflections on the Sea

O billows bounding far,
How wet, how wet ye are!

When first my gaze you met
I said "These waves are wet."

I said it, and am quite
Convinced that I was right.

Who saith that ye are dry?
I give that man the lie.

Thy wetness, O thou sea,
Is wonderful to me.

It agitates my heart,
To think how wet thou art.

No object I have met
Is more profoundly wet.

Methinks 'twere vain to try,
O sea, to wipe thee dry.

I therefore will refrain.
Farewell, thou humid main.

A. E. Housman

Stone Speech

Crowding this beach
are milkstones, white
teardrops; flints
edged out of flinthood
into smoothness chafe
against grainy ovals,
pitted pieces, nosestones,
stoppers and saddles;
veins of orange
inlay black beads:
chalk-swaddled babyshapes,
tiny fists, facestones
and facestone's brother
skullstone, roundheads
pierced by a single eye,
purple finds, all
rubbing shoulders:
a mob of grindings,
groundlings, scatterings
from a million necklaces
mined under sea-hills, the pebbles
are as various as the people.

Charles Tomlinson

The King of Quizzical Island

The King of Quizzical Island
Had a most inquisitive mind.
He said, "If I sail to the edge of the world
I wonder what I'll find?"

His fearful people pleaded.
They wept fat tears of woe.
Some said, "Remain!" and some, "Please stay!"
While others said, "Don't go!"

"For it's quite well known, and I've heard it said
By wise men, old and clever,
That those who sail to the edge of the world
Fall off – and fall for ever."

But the King of Quizzical Island
Said, "Tosh!" and "Bosh!" and "Twaddle!
For I can sail to the edge of the world
As sure as a duck can waddle."

So he built himself a singular ship
Made of wood from the Tea-Bag Tree –
And the rigging was a spider's web
And the rudder a bumble-bee.

The ship sailed out of the harbour
And the silken sails unfurled
As the King of Quizzical Island
Set sail for the edge of the world.

He sailed through waves as high as hills
For thirty days or more
Until at last, the ship was cast
On a higgledy-piggledy shore.

He found himself in a Jigsaw Land
Which lay there, all in pieces:
The blue bits might have been sea – or sky –
Or sheep, with ink-stained fleeces . . .

The green bits might have been grass – or leaves –
Or a snake, or a dragon's tail;
And the white bits might have been clouds – or snow –
Or the teeth of a smiling whale . . .

It took the King nine days and nights
To fit those bits in place –
Then he saw before him a river
And a smile lit up his face.

So he sailed up that Jigsaw River
And there, round the final bend,
He found himself in Vertical Land
Where everything stands on end.

The rivers go up like fountains
And the crocodiles stand on their tails
And the meadows tower like mountains
And the trains run on vertical rails.

The King said, "That's *one* way of using
Every inch of space you've got –
But it doesn't look very comfortable . . ."
And the crocodiles said, "It's not!"

So the singular ship sailed upwards
On a river tall and wide
And from the top of the river
It sailed down the other side.

It sailed through Hurricane Harriet
To the Sea of Dreadful Dreams,
Where the waves are forever wailing,
And the Wild Wind sighs and screams,

Where the Sea-Horse turns into a Night-Mare
And prances upon the foam,
And gaggles of ghostly jelly-fish
Wobble their way back home.

"All things ghastly and ghoulish,"
Said the King, "I can put to flight –
They'll all feel extremely foolish
When I wake, and turn on the light."

He rang a hundred alarm-clocks,
And the Sky switched on the Sun,
And the Dreadful Dreams were ended
As quickly as they'd begun.

The wild wind sank to a whisper
And even the waves were shy
And the moon smiled down, benignly,
From the sleeping deeps of the sky.

The King of Quizzical Island
Sailed on, till he sighted land.
And the singular ship was beached upon
A handy, sandy strand.

He looked at the castle before him,
And knew he had seen it before –
And he said, "I've sailed to the edge of the world,
And arrived at my own back door!"

His people rushed out to greet him –
They gave him a rousing cheer:
And he said, "There *is* no edge of the world –
The world is a perfect sphere.

"I sailed out there in my singular ship,
And I'll tell you what I found.
I found I was back at my own back door –
So I've proved that the world is round!"

Everyone cheered and shouted,
They shouted and cheered and kissed.
Their King had come back from the edge of the world,
And proved it didn't exist!

Gordon Snell

O Sailor, Come Ashore

O Sailor, come ashore,
　　What have you brought for me?
Red coral, white coral,
　　Coral from the sea.

I did not dig it from the ground,
　　Nor pluck it from a tree;
Feeble insects made it
　　In the stormy sea.

Christina Rossetti

The Owl and the Pussy-cat

The Owl and the Pussy-cat went to sea
   In a beautiful pea-green boat,
They took some honey, and plenty of money,
   Wrapped up in a five-pound note.
The Owl looked up to the stars above,
   And sang to a small guitar,
"O lovely Pussy! O Pussy, my love,
    What a beautiful Pussy you are,
      You are,
      You are!
   What a beautiful Pussy you are!"

Pussy said to the Owl, "You elegant fowl!
   How charmingly sweet you sing!
O let us be married! too long we have tarried:
   But what shall we do for a ring?"
They sailed away, for a year and a day,
   To the land where the Bong-tree grows
And there in a wood a Piggy-wig stood
   With a ring at the end of his nose,
      His nose,
      His nose,
   With a ring at the end of his nose.

"Dear Pig, are you willing to sell for one shilling
    Your ring?" Said the Piggy, "I will."
So they took it away, and were married next day
    By the Turkey who lives on the hill.
They dined on mince, and slices of quince,
    Which they ate with a runcible spoon;
And hand in hand, on the edge of the sand,
    They danced by the light of the moon,
            The moon,
            The moon,
They danced by the light of the moon.

Edward Lear

A Ballad of John Silver

We were schooner-rigged and rakish, with a long and lissome hull,
And we flew the pretty colours of the cross-bones and the skull;
We'd a big black Jolly Roger flapping grimly at the fore,
And we sailed the Spanish Water in the happy days of yore.

We'd a long brass gun amidships, like a well-conducted ship,
We had each a brace of pistols and a cutlass at the hip;
It's a point which tells against us, and a fact to be deplored,
But we chased the goodly merchant-men and laid their ships aboard.

Then the dead men fouled the scuppers and the wounded filled the chains,
And the paint-work all was spatter-dashed with other people's brains,
She was boarded, she was looted, she was scuttled till she sank.
And the pale survivors left us by the medium of the plank.

O! then it was (while standing by the taffrail on the poop)
We could hear the drowning folk lament the absent chicken-coop;
Then, having washed the blood away, we'd little else to do
Than to dance a quiet hornpipe as the old salts taught us to.

O! the fiddle on the fo'c's'le, and the slapping naked soles,
And the genial "Down the middle, Jake, and curtsey when she rolls!"
With the silver seas around us and the pale moon overhead,
And the look-out not a-looking and his pipe-bowl glowing red.

Ah! the pig-tailed, quidding pirates and the pretty pranks we played,
All have since been put a stop-to by the naughty Board of Trade;
The schooners and the merry crews are laid away to rest,
A little south the sunset in the Islands of the Blest.

John Masefield

Sir Patrick Spens

I. The Sailing

The king sits in Dunfermline town
    Drinking the blude-red wine;
"O whare will I get a skeely skipper
    To sail this new ship o' mine?"

O up and spak an eldern knight,
    Sat at the king's right knee;
"Sir Patrick Spens is the best sailor
    That ever sail'd the sea."

Our king has written a braid letter,
    And seal'd it with his hand,
And sent it to Sir Patrick Spens,
    Was walking on the strand.

"To Noroway, to Noroway,
    To Noroway o'er the faem;
The king's daughter o' Noroway,
    'Tis thou must bring her hame."

The first word that Sir Patrick read
    So loud, loud laugh'd he;
The neist word that Sir Patrick read
    The tear blinded his e'e.

"O wha is this has done this deed
　　And tauld the king o' me,
To send us out, at this time o' year,
　　To sail upon the sea?

"Be it wind, be it weet, be it hail, be it sleet,
　　Our ship must sail the faem;
The king's daughter o' Noroway,
　　'Tis we must fetch her hame."

They hoysed their sails on Monenday morn
　　Wi' a' the speed they may;
They hae landed in Noroway
　　Upon a Wodensday.

II. The Return

"Mak ready, mak ready, my merry men a'!
　　Our gude ship sails the morn."
"Now ever alack, my master dear,
　　I fear a deadly storm.

"I saw the new moon late yestreen
　　Wi' the auld moon in her arm;
And if we gang to sea, master,
　　I fear we'll come to harm."

They hadna sail'd a league, a league,
  A league but barely three,
When the lift grew dark, and the wind blew loud,
  And gurly grew the sea.

The ankers brak, and the topmast lap,
  It was sic a deadly storm:
And the waves cam owre the broken ship
  Till a' her sides were torn.

"Go fetch a web o' the silken claith,
  Another o' the twine,
And wap them into our ship's side,
  And let nae the sea come in."

They fetch'd a web o' the silken claith,
  Another o' the twine,
And they wapp'd them round that gude ship's side,
  But still the sea came in.

O laith, laith were our gude Scots lords
  To wet their cork-heel'd shoon;
But lang or a' the play was play'd
  They wat their hats aboon.

And mony was the feather bed
   That flatter'd on the faem;
And mony was the gude lord's son
   That never mair cam hame.

O lang, lang may the ladies sit,
   Wi' their fans into their hand,
Before they see Sir Patrick Spens
   Come sailing to the strand!

And lang, lang may the maidens sit
   Wi' their gowd kames in their hair,
A-waiting for their ain dear loves!
   For them they'll see nae mair.

Half-owre, half-owre to Aberdour,
   'Tis fifty fathoms deep;
And there lies gude Sir Patrick Spens,
   Wi' the Scots lords at his feet!

Anon

Skeely means skilful; the lift is the sky;
lap means split; flatter'd means floated;
kames are combs.

A Sea Dirge

Full fathom five thy father lies:
    Of his bones are coral made;
Those are pearls that were his eyes:
    Nothing of him that doth fade,
But doth suffer a sea-change
Into something rich and strange.
Sea-nymphs hourly ring his knell:
Hark! now I hear them –
    Ding, dong, bell.

William Shakespeare

The Jumblies

They went to sea in a Sieve, they did,
    In a Sieve they went to sea:
In spite of all their friends could say,
On a winter's morn, on a stormy day,
    In a Sieve they went to sea!
And when the Sieve turned round and round,
And every one cried, "You'll all be drowned!"
They called aloud, "Our Sieve ain't big,
But we don't care a button! we don't care a fig!
    In a Sieve we'll go to sea!"
      Far and few, far and few,
        Are the lands where the Jumblies live;
        Their heads are green, and their hands are blue,
        And they went to sea in a Sieve.

They sailed away in a Sieve, they did,
   In a Sieve they sailed so fast,
With only a beautiful pea-green veil
Tied with a riband by way of a sail,
   To a small tobacco-pipe mast;
And every one said, who saw them go,
"O won't they be soon upset, you know!
For the sky is dark, and the voyage is long,
And happen what may, it's extremely wrong
   In a Sieve to sail so fast!"
     Far and few, far and few,
       Are the lands where the Jumblies live;
       Their heads are green, and their hands are blue,
       And they went to sea in a Sieve.

The water it soon came in, it did,
   The water it soon came in;
So to keep them dry, they wrapped their feet
In a pinky paper all folded neat,
   And they fastened it down with a pin.
And they passed the night in a crockery-jar,
And each of them said, "How wise we are!
Though the sky be dark, and the voyage be long,
Yet we never can think we were rash or wrong,
   While round in our Sieve we spin!"
     Far and few, far and few,
       Are the lands where the Jumblies live;
       Their heads are green, and their hands are blue,
       And they went to sea in a Sieve.

And all night long they sailed away;
    And when the sun went down,
They whistled and warbled a moony song
To the echoing sound of a coppery gong,
    In the shade of the mountains brown.
"O Timballo! How happy we are,
When we live in a sieve and a crockery-jar,
And all night long in the moonlight pale,
We sail away with a pea-green sail,
    In the shade of the mountains brown!"
      Far and few, far and few,
        Are the lands where the Jumblies live;
        Their heads are green, and their hands are blue,
        And they went to sea in a Sieve.

They sailed to the Western Sea, they did,
    To a land all covered with trees,
And they bought an Owl, and a useful Cart,
And a pound of Rice, and a Cranberry Tart,
    And a hive of silvery Bees.
And they bought a Pig, and some green Jack-daws,
And a lovely Monkey with lollipop paws,
And forty bottles of Ring-Bo-Ree,
    And no end of Stilton Cheese.
      Far and few, far and few,
        Are the lands where the Jumblies live;
        Their heads are green, and their hands are blue,
        And they went to sea in a Sieve.

And in twenty years they all came back,
    In twenty years or more,
And every one said, "How tall they've grown!
For they've been to the Lakes, and the Torrible Zone,
    And the hills of the Chankly Bore";
And they drank their health, and gave them a feast
Of dumplings made of beautiful yeast;
And every one said, "If we only live,
We too will go to sea in a Sieve –
    To the hills of the Chankly Bore!"
      Far and few, far and few,
        Are the lands where the Jumblies live;
        Their heads are green, and their hands are blue,
        And they went to sea in a Sieve.

Edward Lear

The Spellbound Mountain

Golden Dreams and Fiery Nightmares
Magical People and Enchanted Places

Romance

When I was but thirteen or so
   I went into a golden land,
Chimborazo, Cotopaxi
   Took me by the hand.

My father died, my brother too,
   They passed like fleeting dreams.
I stood where Popocatapetl
   In the sunlight gleams.

I dimly heard the Master's voice
   And boys far-off at play,
Chimborazo, Cotopaxi
   Had stolen me away.

I walked in a great golden dream
   To and fro from school –
Shining Popocatapetl
   The dusty streets did rule.

I walked home with a gold dark boy
   And never a word I'd say,
Chimborazo, Cotopaxi
   Had taken my speech away:

I gazed entranced upon his face
    Fairer than any flower –
O shining Popocatapetl
    It was thy magic hour:

The houses, people, traffic seemed
    Thin fading dreams by day,
Chimborazo, Cotopaxi
    They had stolen my soul away!

Walter James Turner

The Aristocrat

The Devil is a gentleman, and asks you down to stay
At his little place at What'sitsname (it isn't far away).
They say the sport is splendid; there is always something new,
And fairy scenes, and fearful feats that none but he can do;
He can shoot the feathered cherubs if they fly on the estate,
Or fish for Father Neptune with the mermaids for a bait;
He scaled amid the staggering stars that precipice, the sky,
And blew his trumpet above heaven, and got by mastery
The starry crown of God Himself, and shoved it on the shelf;
But the Devil is a gentleman, and doesn't brag himself.

O blind your eyes and break your heart and hack your hand away,
And lose your love and shave your head; but do not go to stay
At the little place in What'sitsname where folks are rich and clever;
The golden and the goodly house, where things grow worse for ever;
There are things you need not know of, though you live and die in vain
There are souls more sick of pleasure than you are sick of pain;
There is a game of April Fool that's played behind its door,
Where the fool remains for ever and the April comes no more,
Where the splendour of the daylight grows drearier than the dark,
And life droops like a vulture that once was such a lark:
And that is the Blue Devil that once was the Blue Bird;
For the Devil is a gentleman, and doesn't keep his word.

G. K. Chesterton

Kubla Khan

In Xanadu did Kubla Khan
    A stately pleasure-dome decree:
Where Alph, the sacred river, ran
Through caverns measureless to man
    Down to a sunless sea.
    So twice five miles of fertile ground
    With walls and towers were girdled round:
And there were gardens bright with sinuous rills
Where blossom'd many an incense-bearing tree;
And here were forests ancient as the hills,
Enfolding sunny spots of greenery.

But O, that deep romantic chasm which slanted
Down the green hill athwart a cedarn cover!
A savage place! as holy and enchanted
As e'er beneath a waning moon was haunted
By woman wailing for her demon-lover!
And from this chasm, with ceaseless turmoil seething,
As if this earth in fast thick pants were breathing,
A mighty fountain momently was forced;
Amid whose swift half-intermitted burst
Huge fragments vaulted like rebounding hail,
Or chaffy grain beneath the thresher's flail:
And 'mid these dancing rocks at once and ever
It flung up momently the sacred river.
Five miles meandering with a mazy motion
Through wood and dale the sacred river ran,
Then reach'd the caverns measureless to man,
And sank in tumult to a lifeless ocean:
And 'mid this tumult Kubla heard from far
Ancestral voices prophesying war!

The shadow of the dome of pleasure
 Floated midway on the waves;
Where was heard the mingled measure
 From the fountain and the caves.
It was a miracle of rare device,
A sunny pleasure-dome with caves of ice!

A damsel with a dulcimer
 In a vision once I saw:
It was an Abyssinian maid,
 And on her dulcimer she play'd,
Singing of Mount Abora.
Could I revive within me,
 Her symphony and song,
To such a deep delight 'twould win me,
That with music loud and long,
I would build that dome in air,
That sunny dome! those caves of ice!
And all who heard should see them there,
And all should cry, Beware! Beware!
His flashing eyes, his floating hair!
Weave a circle round him thrice,
 And close your eyes with holy dread,
 For he on honey-dew hath fed,
And drunk the milk of Paradise.

Samuel Taylor Coleridge

Science Fiction — Contribution to the Shakespeare Festival

Dragon-lovers with sweet serious eyes
brood in a desert wood thick with bluebells:
the tough, fire-belching curiosities
mate among ugly smoke and pungent smells.

Seal women linger on the wild foreshore
where in the wrack and footprints of green slime
doe-eyed enormous weed-eaters explore
pebbles and sand, and then begin to climb.

I belong to the Monster Society,
they are my only ramshackle heroes,
I really love them, and whenever I see
monster films I cheer them from the back rows.

I like steam tractors and big, broken machines,
have two old coke bottles on my book-shelf,
I sit through Shakespeare mostly for the scenes
where I am Caliban and love myself.

Peter Levi

Jerusalem

And did those feet in ancient time
    Walk upon England's mountains green?
And was the holy Lamb of God
    On England's pleasant pastures seen?

And did the Countenance Divine
    Shine forth upon our clouded hills?
And was Jerusalem builded here
    Among these dark Satanic Mills?

Bring me my bow of burning gold!
    Bring me my arrows of desire!
Bring me my spear! O clouds, unfold!
    Bring me my chariot of fire!

I will not cease from mental fight,
    Nor shall my sword sleep in my hand,
Till we have built Jerusalem
    In England's green and pleasant land.

William Blake

Things

There are worse things than having behaved foolishly in public.
There are worse things than these miniature betrayals,
committed or endured or suspected; there are worse things
than not being able to sleep for thinking about them.
It is 5 a.m. All the worse things come stalking in
and stand icily about the bed looking worse and worse
                                        and worse.

Fleur Adcock

Griffin of the Night

I'm holding my son in my arms
sweating after nightmares
small me
fingers in his mouth
his other fist clenched in my hair
small me
sweating after nightmares

Michael Ondaatje

Imagine

Imagine there's no heaven
It's easy if you try.
No hell below us,
Above us only sky.
Imagine all the people,
Living for today.

Imagine there's no countries
It isn't hard to do,
Nothing to kill or die for
And no religion too.
Imagine all the people
Living life in peace.
You may say I'm a dreamer,
But I'm not the only one.
I hope some day you'll join us
And the world will be as one.

Imagine no possessions
I wonder if you can
No need for greed or hunger
A brotherhood of man.
Imagine all the people
Sharing all the world.
You may say I'm a dreamer,
But I'm not the only one.
I hope some day you'll join us
And the world will live as one.

John Lennon

The Witch! The Witch!

The Witch! the Witch! don't let her get you!
Or your Aunt wouldn't know you the next time
she met you!

Eleanor Farjeon

Alison Gross

O Alison Gross, that lives in yon tow'r,
  The ugliest witch i' the north countrie,
Has trysted me ae day up till her bow'r
  And mony fair speeches she made to me.

She straik'd my head an' she kaim'd my hair,
  An' she set me down saftly on her knee;
Says, "Gin ye will be my lemman sae true,
  Sae mony braw things as I would you gie!"

She show'd me a mantle o' red scarlét,
  Wi' gouden flowers an' fringes fine;
Says, "Gin ye will be my lemman sae true,
  This gudely gift it sall be thine" –

"Awa', awa', ye ugly witch,
  Haud far awa', an' lat me be!
I never will be your lemman sae true,
  An' I wish I were out o' your company."

She neist brought a sark o' the saftest silk,
  Well wrought wi' pearls about the band,
Says, "Gin ye will be my lemman sae true,
  This gudely gift ye sall command."

She show'd me a cup o' the good red gowd,
    Well set wi' jewels sae fair to see;
Says, "Gin ye will be my lemman sae true,
    This gudely gift I will you gie" –

"Awa', awa', ye ugly witch,
    Haud far awa', an' lat me be!
For I wouldna once kiss your ugly mouth
    For a' the gifts that ye could gie."

She's turn'd her right an' roun' about,
    An' thrice she blaw on a grass-green horn;
An' she sware by the moon an' the stars abune
    That she'd gar me rue the day I was born.

Then out has she ta'en a silver wand,
    An' she's turn'd her three times roun' and roun';
She mutter'd sic words till my strength it fail'd,
    An' I fell down senseless upon the groun'.

She's turn'd me into an ugly worm,
    And gar'd me toddle about the tree;
An' ay, on ilka Saturday's night,
    My sister Maisry came to me.

Wi' silver bason an' silver kaim
    To kaim my headie upon her knee;
But or I had kiss'd wi' Alison Gross
    I'd sooner ha' toddled about the tree.

But as it fell out, on last Hallowe'en,
    When the Seely Court was ridin' by,
The Queen lighted down on a gowany bank
    Nae far frae the tree where I wont to lye.

She took me up in her milk-white han',
    An' she's straik'd me three times o'er her knee;
She changed me again to my ain proper shape,
    An' nae mair I toddle about the tree.

Anon

Trysted means invited; a lemman is a sweetheart;
Seely Court is the Happy Court (of the Fairies);
gowany means daisied.

La Belle Dame Sans Merci

O what can ail thee, knight-at-arms,
　　Alone and palely loitering?
The sedge has wither'd from the lake,
　　And no birds sing.

O what can ail thee, knight-at-arms,
　　So haggard and so woe-begone?
The squirrel's granary is full,
　　And the harvest's done.

I see a lily on thy brow,
　　With anguish moist and fever dew;
And on thy cheeks a fading rose
　　Fast withereth too.

I met a lady in the meads,
　　Full beautiful – a faery's child;
Her hair was long, her foot was light,
　　And her eyes were wild.

I made a garland for her head,
　　And bracelets too, and fragrant zone;
She look'd at me as she did love,
　　And made sweet moan.

I set her on my pacing steed,
　　And nothing else saw all day long;
For sidelong would she bend, and sing
　　A faery's song.

She found me roots of relish sweet,
    And honey wild, and manna-dew;
And sure in language strange she said,
    "I love thee true."

She took me to her elfin grot,
    And there she wept and sigh'd full sore:
And there I shut her wild, wild eyes
    With kisses four.

And there she lulled me asleep,
    And there I dream'd – Ah! woe betide.
The latest dream I ever dream'd
    On the cold hill's side.

I saw pale kings and princes too,
    Pale warriors – death-pale were they all;
They cried, "La Belle Dame Sans Merci
    Hath thee in thrall!"

I saw their starv'd lips in the gloam,
    With horrid warning gaped wide;
And I awoke, and found me here
    On the cold hill's side.

And this is why I sojourn here,
    Alone and palely loitering;
Though the sedge is wither'd from the lake,
    And no birds sing.

John Keats

The Woman of Water

There once was a woman of water
Refused a Wizard her hand.
So he took the tears of a statue
And the weight from a grain of sand
And he squeezed the sap from a comet
And the height from a cypress tree
And he drained the dark from midnight
And he charmed the brains from a bee
And he soured the mixture with thunder
And stirred it with ice from hell
And the woman of water drank it down
And she changed into a well.

There once was a woman of water
Who was changed into a well
And the well smiled up at the Wizard
And down down down that old Wizard fell . . .

Adrian Mitchell

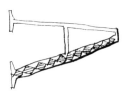

Beware :   Do Not Read This Poem

tonite, thriller was
abt an ol woman, so vain she
surrounded herself w/
        many mirrors

it got so bad that finally she
locked herself indoors & her
whole life became the
        mirrors

one day the villagers broke
into her house   ,   but she was too
swift for them   .   she disappeared
        into a mirror
each tenant who bought the house
after that   ,   lost a loved one to

        the ol woman in the mirror   :
        first a little girl
        then a young woman
        then   the   young   woman/s   husband

the hunger of this poem is legendary
it has taken in many victims
back off from this poem
it has drawn in yr feet
back off from this poem
it has drawn in yr legs

back off from this poem

it is a greedy mirror

you are into this poem   .   from

      the waist down

nobody can hear you can they?

this poem has had you up to here

      belch

this poem aint got no manners

you cant call out frm this poem

relax now & go w/ this poem

move & roll on to this poem

do not resist this poem

this poem has yr eyes

this poem has his head

this poem has his arms

this poem has his fingers

this poem has his fingertips

this poem is the reader & the

reader this poem

statistic   :   the us bureau of missing persons re-

      ports that in 1968 over 100,000 people

      disappeared leaving no solid clues

      nor trace   only

a space   in the lives of their friends

Ishmael Reed

Warning to Children

Children, if you dare to think
Of the greatness, rareness, muchness,
Fewness of this precious only
Endless world in which you say
You live, you think of things like this:
Blocks of slate enclosing dappled
Red and green, enclosing tawny
Yellow nets, enclosing white
And black acres of dominoes,
Where a neat brown paper parcel
Tempts you to untie the string.
In the parcel a small island,
On the island a large tree,
On the tree a husky fruit.
Strip the husk and pare the rind off:
In the kernel you will see
Blocks of slate enclosed by dappled
Red and green, enclosed by tawny
Yellow nets, enclosed by white
And black acres of dominoes,
Where the same brown paper parcel –
Children, leave the string untied!
For who dares undo the parcel
Finds himself at once inside it,
On the island, in the fruit,
Blocks of slate about his head,
Finds himself enclosed by dappled
Green and red, enclosed by yellow
Tawny nets, enclosed by black
And white acres of dominoes,

With the same brown paper parcel
Still untied upon his knee.
And, if he then should dare to think
Of the fewness, muchness, rareness,
Greatness of this endless only
Precious world in which he says
He lives – he then unties the string.

Robert Graves

Silver

Slowly, silently, now the moon
Walks the night in her silver shoon;
This way, and that, she peers, and sees
Silver fruit upon silver trees;
One by one the casements catch
Her beams beneath the silvery thatch;
Couched in his kennel, like a log,
With paws of silver sleeps the dog;
From their shadowy cote the white breasts peep
Of doves in a silver-feathered sleep;
A harvest mouse goes scampering by,
With silver claws, and silver eye;
And moveless fish in the water gleam,
By silver reeds in a silver stream.

Walter de la Mare

The Old Summerhouse

This blue-washed, old, thatched summerhouse –
Paint scaling, and fading from its walls –
How often from its hingeless door
I have watched – dead leaf, like the ghost of a mouse,
Rasping the worn brick floor –
The snows of the weir descending below,
And their thunderous waterfall.

Fall – fall: dark, garrulous rumour,
Until I could listen no more.
Could listen no more – for beauty with sorrow
Is a burden hard to be borne:
The evening light on the foam, and the swans, there;
That music, remote, forlorn.

Walter de la Mare

The Negro Speaks of Rivers

I've known rivers:
I've known rivers ancient as the world and older than the flow
    of human blood in human veins.

My soul has grown deep like the rivers.

I bathed in the Euphrates when dawns were young.
I built my hut near the Congo and it lulled me to sleep.
I looked upon the Nile and raised the pyramids above it.
I heard the singing of the Mississippi when Abe Lincoln went
    down to New Orleans, and I've seen its muddy bosom turn
    all golden in the sunset.

I've known rivers:
Ancient, dusky rivers.

My soul has grown deep like the rivers.

Langston Hughes

Weeds

Some people are flower lovers.
I'm a weed lover.

Weeds don't need planting in well-drained soil;
They don't ask for fertiliser or bits of rag to scare
    away birds
They come without invitation;
And they don't take the hint when you want them to go.
Weeds are nobody's guests:
More like squatters.

Coltsfoot laying claim to every new-dug clump of clay;
Pearlwort scraping up a living from a ha'porth of
    mortar;
Dandelions you daren't pick or you know what will
    happen;
Sour docks that make a first-rate poultice for nettle-
    stings;
And flat-foot plantain in the back street,
    gathering more dust than the dustmen.

Even the names are a folk-song:
Fat hen, rat's tail, cat's ear, old men's baccy and
    Stinking Billy
Ring a prettier chime for me than honeysuckle or
    jasmine,
And Sweet Cicely smells cleaner than Sweet William
    though
    she's barred from the garden.

And they have their uses, weeds.
Think of the old, worked-out mines –
Quarries and tunnels, earth scorched and scruffy,
    torn-up railways, splintered sleepers,
And a whole Sahara of grit and smother and cinders.

But go in summer and where is all the clutter?
For a new town has risen of a thousand towers,
Sparkling like granite, swaying like larches,
And every spiky belfry humming with a peal of bees.
Rosebay willowherb:
Only a weed!

Flowers are for wrapping in cellophane to present as a
    bouquet;
Flowers are for prize-arrangements in vases and silver
    tea-pots;
Flowers are for plaiting into funeral wreaths.
You can keep your flowers.
Give me weeds!

Norman Nicholson

Arracombe Wood

Some said, because he wud'n spaik
Any words to women but Yes and No,
Nor put out his hand for Parson to shake
He mun be bird-witted. But I do go
By the lie of the barley that he did sow,
And I wish no better thing than to hold a rake
Like Dave, in his time, or to see him mow.

Put up in churchyard a month ago,
"A bitter old soul," they said, but it wadn't so.
His heart were in Arracombe Wood where he'd used to go
To sit and talk wi' his shadder till sun went low,
Though what it was all about us'll never know.
And there baint no mem'ry in the place
Of th' old man's footmark, nor his face;
Arracombe Wood do think more of a crow –
'Will be violets there in the Spring: in Summer time the spider's lace;
And come the Fall, the whizzle and race
Of the dry, dead leaves when the wind gies chase;
And on the Eve of Christmas, fallin' snow.

Charlotte Mew

Blow, Bugle, Blow

The splendour falls on castle walls
And snowy summits old in story:
The long light shakes across the lakes,
And the wild cataract leaps in glory.
Blow, bugle, blow, set the wild echoes flying,
Blow, bugle; answer, echoes, dying, dying, dying.

O hark, O hear! how thin and clear,
And thinner, clearer, farther going!
O sweet and far from cliff and scar
The horns of Elfland faintly blowing!
Blow, let us hear the purple glens replying:
Blow, bugle; answer, echoes, dying, dying, dying.

O love, they die in yon rich sky,
They faint on hill or field or river:
Our echoes roll from soul to soul,
And grow for ever and for ever.
Blow, bugle, blow, set the wild echoes flying,
And answer, echoes, answer, dying, dying, dying.

Alfred, Lord Tennyson

Speak of the North

Speak of the North! A lonely moor
Silent and dark and trackless swells,
The waves of some wild streamlet pour
Hurriedly through its ferny dells.

Profoundly still the twilight air,
Lifeless the landscape; so we deem
Till like a phantom gliding near
A stag bends down to drink the stream.

And far away a mountain zone,
A cold, white waste of snow-drifts lies,
And one star, large and soft and lone,
Silently lights the unclouded skies.

Charlotte Brontë

The Trees Are Down

— and he cried with a loud voice:
Hurt not the earth, neither the sea, nor the trees —
(Revelation)

They are cutting down the great plane trees at the end of the gardens.
For days there has been the grate of the saw, the swish of the branches as they fall,
The crash of trunks, the rustle of trodden leaves,
With the "Whoops" and the "Whoas", the loud common talk, the loud common laughs of the men, above it all.

I remember one evening of a long past spring
Turning in at a gate, getting out of a cart, and finding a large dead rat in the mud of the drive.
I remember thinking: alive or dead, a rat was a god-forsaken thing,
But at least, in May, that even a rat should be alive.

The week's work here is as good as done. There is just one bough
  On the roped bole, in the fine grey rain,
      Green and high
      And lonely against the sky.
        (Down now! –)
      And but for that,
      If an old dead rat
Did once, for a moment, unmake the spring, I might never have thought of
him again.

It is not for a moment the spring is unmade today;
These were great trees, it was in them from root to stem:
When the men with the "Whoops" and the "Whoas" have carted the whole of
the whispering loveliness away
Half the spring, for me, will have gone with them.

It is going now, and my heart has been struck with the hearts of the planes;
Half my life it has beat with these, in the sun, in the rains,
      In the March wind, the May breeze,
In the great gales that came over to them across the roofs from the great seas.
      There was only a quiet rain when they were dying;
      They must have heard the sparrows flying,
And the small creeping creatures in the earth where they were lying –
      But I, all day, I heard an angel crying:
        "Hurt not the trees."

Charlotte Mew

Lucy in the Sky with Diamonds

Picture yourself in a boat on a river,
with tangerine trees and marmalade skies.
Somebody calls you, you answer quite slowly,
a girl with kaleidoscope eyes.
Cellophane flowers of yellow and green,
towering over your head.
Look for the girl with the sun in her eyes,
and she's gone.
Lucy in the sky with diamonds,
Follow her down to a bridge by a fountain
where rocking horse people eat marshmallow pies,
everyone smiles as you drift past the flowers,
that grow so incredibly high.
Newspaper taxis appear on the shore,
waiting to take you away.
Climb in the back with your head in the clouds,
and you're gone.
Lucy in the sky with diamonds,
Picture yourself on a train in a station,
with plasticine porters with looking-glass ties,
suddenly someone is there at the turnstile,
the girl with kaleidoscope eyes.
Lucy in the sky with diamonds.

John Lennon and Paul McCartney

Song in Space

When man first flew beyond the sky
He looked back into the world's blue eye.
Man said: What makes your eye so blue?
Earth said: The tears in the oceans do.
Why are the seas so full of tears?
Because I've wept so many thousand years.
Why do you weep as you dance through space?
Because I am the Mother of the Human Race.

Adrian Mitchell

Autumn

In autumn I cannot believe my eyes the leaves turn yellow and red. The fresh beautiful airy smell I cannot avoid. I hear my steps go crash crunch. Oh why can't autumn be so long. I like the sound of trees in the wind, so sweet are the animals of this park. I dare not pick the high red mushrooms. The squirrels are the King of autumn. The berries hang glowing bright red and no people seem to run about. But autumn is my lucky season. The fire is bright burning red as night-time falls. I like to sit and tell the tale of autumn falling on the rail. Oh please do not let autumn go. That wicked noise of Hallowe'en. Good-bye pretty blue peck birds but no good-bye to autumn fall. That wicked man can say good-bye by falling down in ashes high. The clock goes forward just swing swing swing. I get up and say it's dark dark dark. I like to dream of autumn season. The people get wrapped up warm in scarves and jackets of soft white wool but I wear more than just one thing. I wear three pairs of woolly white socks. The animals hibernate in small brown nests. I pretend to be a little bird just one step in my nest.

Marina Plentl

Pleasant Sounds

The rustling of leaves under the feet in woods and under hedges;

The crumping of cat-ice and snow down wood-rides, narrow
lanes, and every street causeway;

Rustling through a wood or rather rushing, while the wind
halloos in the oak-top like thunder;

The rustle of birds' wings startled from their nests or flying
unseen into the bushes;

The whizzing of larger birds overhead in a wood, such as crows,
puddocks, buzzards;

The trample of robins and woodlarks on the brown leaves, and
the patter of squirrels on the green moss;

The fall of an acorn on the ground, the pattering of nuts on the
hazel branches as they fall from ripeness;

The flirt of the groundlark's wing from the stubbles – how
sweet such pictures on dewy mornings, when the dew
flashes from its brown feathers!

John Clare

Be a Butterfly

Don't be a kyatta-pilla
Be a butterfly
old preacher screamed
to illustrate his sermon
of Jesus and the higher life

rivulets of well-earned
sweat sliding down
his muscly mahogany face
in the half-empty school church
we sat shaking with muffling
laughter
watching our mother trying to save
herself from joining the wave

only our father remaining poker face
and afterwards we always went home to
split peas Sunday soup
with dumplings, fufu and pigtail

Don't be a kyatta-pilla
Be a butterfly
Be a butterfly

That was de life preacher
and you was right

Grace Nichols

Blow the Stars Home

Blow the Stars home, Wind, blow the Stars home
Ere Morning drowns them in golden foam.

Eleanor Farjeon

Night Way

In beauty	may I walk
All day long	may I walk
Through the returning seasons	may I walk
Beautifully will I possess again	
Beautifully birds	
Beautifully joyful birds	
On the trail marked with pollen	may I walk
With grasshoppers about my feet	may I walk
With dew about my feet	may I walk
With beauty	may I walk
With beauty before me	may I walk
With beauty behind me	may I walk
With beauty above me	may I walk
With beauty all around me	may I walk
In old age, wandering on a trail of beauty, lively,	may I walk
In old age, wandering on a trail of beauty, living again,	may I walk
It is finished in beauty	
It is finished in beauty	

Anon

(translated from the Navajo by Jerome K. Rothenberg)

ACKNOWLEDGEMENTS

'Things' by Fleur Adcock from SELECTED POEMS, reprinted by permission of Oxford University Press; By kind permission of John Agard c/o Caroline Sheldon Literary Agency 'Don't Call Alligator Long Mouth Till You Cross River' from SAY IT AGAIN GRANNY published by Cambridge University Press 1986; 'The Justice of the Peace' by Hilaire Belloc reprinted by permission of the Peters Fraser and Dunlop Group Ltd; 'Fantasy of an African Boy' © copyright 1981 James Berry; 'White Child Meets Black Man' from FRACTURED CIRCLES by James Berry, published by New Beacon Books in 1979; 'Go to Ahmedabad' and 'Maninagar Days' by Sujata Bhatt from MONKEY SHADOWS AND BRUNIZEM, published by Carcanet Press Limited; 'After Prevert' and 'Seven Activities for a Young Child' by Alan Brownjohn, reprinted by permission of Rosica Colin Limited; 'Figgie Hobbin' by Charles Causley, from FIGGIE HOBBIN published by Macmillan, reprinted by permission of David Higham Associates; 'Happiest Girl' © copyright 1982 Frances Mary Whittle, née Clewlow; 'Alternative Endings to an Unwritten Ballad' by Paul Dehn from DANCE MACABRE, reprinted by permission of London Management; 'Comprehensive' by Carol Ann Duffy from STANDING FEMALE NUDE, published by Anvil Press Poetry (1985); 'A Hard Rain's a-Gonna Fall' by Bob Dylan, reprinted by permission of Special Rider Music/ Sony Music Publishing, 17/19 Soho Square, London W1V 6HE; 'Lion and Albert' words by George Marriott Edgar copyright © 1968, reproduced by permission of Francis Day and Hunter Ltd, London WC2H 0EA; 'Skimbleshanks: the Railway Cat' by TS Eliot from OLD POSSUM'S BOOK OF PRACTICAL CATS, reprinted by permission of Faber and Faber Limited; 'Blow the Stars Home'. 'It Was Long Ago' and 'The Witch! The Witch!' by Eleanor Farjeon from SILVER, SAND AND SNOW published by Michael Joseph, reprinted by permission of David Higham Associates; 'Starting to Make a Tree' copyright © Roy Fisher 1998. Reprinted from POEMS 1955 – 1987 by Roy Fisher (1988) by permission of Oxford University Press; 'Song: Lift-Boy' and 'Warning to Children' by Robert Graves from COLLECTED POEMS 1975, reprinted by permission of A. P. Watt Ltd on behalf of The Trustees of The Robert Graves Copyright Trust; 'Without You' © Adrian Henri 1986 from COLLECTED POEMS published by Allison and Busby and reprinted by permission of Rogers Coleridge and White Ltd; 'Message From the Border' © 1962, 1992 by Anselm Hollo, originally published in AND IT IS A SONG, Migrant Press, Worcester/England and Ventura/California, 1965' 'In Painswick Churchyard' by Frances Horovitz: COLLECTED POEMS (Bloodaxe Books and Enitharmon Press, 1985); 'Look Ahead' © Michael Horovitz, published in GROWING UP: SELECTED POEMS AND PICTURES 1951-1979 (Allison and Busby 1979); 'Centrifugalized in Finsbury Park' © Libby Houston 1981, reprinted from AT THE MERCY (Allison and Busby 1981) by permission of Libby Houston; 'Rotting Song' © Libby Houston 1971, reprinted from PLAIN CLOTHES (Allison and Busby 1981) by permission of Libby Houston; 'The Negro Speaks of Rivers' by Langston Hughes reprinted from SELECTED POEMS published by Vintage, by permission of David Higham Associates; 'Cow'; by Ted Hughes from THE CAT AND THE CUCKOO, published by and reprinted by permission of Faber and Faber Limited; 'The Warm and the Cold' by Ted Hughes from SEASON SONGS, published by and reprinted by permission of Faber and Faber Limited; 'Where Poems Come From' © Nigel Jenkins, from SONG AND DANCE (Poetry Wales Press 1981) and ACTS OF UNION SELECTED POEMS 1974 – 1989 (Gwasg Gomer, 1990); 'Reggae Sounds' by Linton Kwesi Johnson, reprinted by permission of LKJ Music Publishers Ltd; 'Hard Times Ain't Gone Nowhere' by Lonnie Johnson from BLUES AND THE POETIC SPIRIT by Paul Garon (1975); 'About Friends' by Brian Jones from A SPITFIRE ON THE NORTHERN LINE, published by Chatto and Windus and reprinted

SELECTED POEMS published by Routledge, 1988; 'Jungle Husband' by Stevie Smith from THE COLLECTED POEMS OF STEVIE SMITH (PENGUIN 20TH CENTURY CLASSICS) and reprinted by permission of James MacGibbon; 'The King of Quizzical Island' by Gordon Snell, published by and reprinted by permission of JOHN JOHNSON (authors agent) LIMITED; 'All Over the World' © Dr Christina Starobin; '1945' by Geoffrey Summerfield from WELCOME, published by Andre Deutsch and reprinted by permission of Scholastic Publications Ltd; 'Fern Hill' by Dylan Thomas from THE POEMS, published by Dent and reprinted by permission of David Higham Associates; 'Stone Speech' by Charles Tomlinson from COLLECTED POEMS (1985), reprinted by permission of Oxford University Press; 'The Lion' and 'Romance' by W J Turner from SELECTED POEMS 1916 – 36, published by Oxford University Press; 'As the Cat' 'The Dance' and 'To a Poor Old Woman' by William Carlos Williams from THE COLLECTED POEMS, reprinted by permission of Carcanet Press Ltd; 'Grandad' by Kit Wright from RABBITTING ON, published by Fontana Lions, an imprint of HarperCollins Publishers and reprinted by permission of HarperCollins Publishers; 'Greedyguts' by Kit Wright from HOTDOG AND OTHER STORIES copyright © Kit Wright 1981, published by Viking Kestrel and Puffin Books.

Index *of* Poets

INDEX OF POETS

Norman MacCaig, 1910–, 112, 134, 193

Paul McCartney, 1942–, 112, 269

Roger McGough, 1937–, 21

John Masefield, 1878–1967, 227

Charlotte Mew, 1870–1928, 166, 264, 267

Robert Mezey, 1935–, 86

Roger Miller, 167

Spike Milligan, 1919–, 80, 184

Adrian Mitchell, 1932–, 254, 270

Egbert Moore, 97

Edwin Morgan, 1920–, 192

Grace Nichols, 1950–, 43, 273

Norman Nicholson, 1914–, 262

Michael Ondaatje, 1943–, 110, 246

Wilfred Owen, 1893–1918, 162

Brian Patten, 1946–, 62, 133, 170, 198

Mervyn Peake, 1911–68, 176, 177, 215

Marina Plentl, 271

Mauricio Redoles, 36

Ishmael Reed, 1938–, 255

Jeremy Reed, 1951–, 100

Theodore Roethke, 1908–63, 146

Michael Rosen, 1946–, 151

Christina Rossetti, 1830–94, 18, 52, 174, 194, 224

William Shakespeare, 1564-1616, 59, 73, 233

Percy Bysshe Shelley, 1792–1822, 197

Sir Philip Sidney, 1554–86, 48

Jon Silkin, 1930–, 142

Stevie Smith, 1902–71, 196

Gordon Snell, 219

Christina Starobin, 160

Robert Louis Stevenson, 1850–94, 61

Geoffrey Summerfield, 24

Alfred, Lord Tennyson, 1809–92, 111, 118, 139, 265

Dylan Thomas, 1914–53, 32

Charles Tomlinson, 218

Walter James Turner, 1889–1946, 135, 238

Walt Whitman, 1819–92, 57, 104, 144

William Carlos Williams, 1883–1963, 76, 99, 107

Kit Wright, 1944–, 55, 78

W. B. Yeats, 1868–1939, 60, 93

INDEX *of* FIRST LINES

INDEX OF FIRST LINES

When I was bound apprentice, in famous Lincolnshire, 164

When I was but thirteen or so, 238

When I went to the circus that had pitched on the waste lot, 95

When icicles hang by the wall, 73

When man first flew beyond the sky, 270

When midnight comes a host of dogs and men, 126

"Where have you been all the day", 210

Where the city's ceaseless crowd moves on, the live-long day, 144

Where were the greenhouses going, 146

While going the road to sweet Athy, 84

While playing at the woodland's edge, 198

White bird, featherless, 175

Why is there no monument, 80

Without you every morning would be like going back to work after a holiday, 39

Women are knitting, 160

Yea, the coneys are scared by the thud of hoofs, 81